Miracle in a Mill

PAUL HENCZEL

Written by Paul Henczel
Edited by Kristin van Vloten, Salvo Communications
Forward by Paul Petrie
Cover Design by Agata Klein, Gold Leaf Graphic Design
Artist sketches by Trish Rapske
Cover image: Stock photo ID: 63445681
Published by Affective Communications

Canada:
Affective Communications
PO Box 813 Stn A
#30 – 32500 South Fraser Way
Abbotsford, BC
V2T 7A2
paul@miracleinamill.com
www.miracleinamill.com

ISBN-13: 978-1535177405
ISBN-10: 1535177403

DEDICATION

I dedicate this book to my wife Jennifer Henczel, and my children Ashleigh and Nathan. Your love and support over the years has inspired me to be a better person, as I spent time recovering, learning, and writing. To my friend Ron who tragically passed away 11 months after my accident. I think of you daily; your time with us was short, yet sweet. Love you, Bra! Also, to the Dunkley's, Paul Petrie, friends, and the Connect Now Community. Thank you for your support and encouragement, I love all of you!

CONTENTS

ACKNOWLEDGMENTS

I want to say a special thank you to some incredible people who helped make this book possible.

Thank you to my loving wife Jennifer, who has stood by me consistently from day one. Your support, patience, and love has been unwavering. You have stayed right beside me through my best and worst, while gently challenging me along the way. Your integrity and strength motivates me hour by hour, and I literally would not be where I am without you. You are the best and smartest person I have ever met. You make me happy and laugh every day. I love you!

To our two children, Ashleigh and Nathan, for inspiring me daily; words could never express how I feel about you. I am so proud to be your dad, and see you both grow into amazing people. You are the best kids anyone could possibly dream of having. You were so strong through all of this, and that in turn helped me be stronger. I love you!

Thank you so much to all those who helped rescue me; I wouldn't be here without them and their heroic efforts. Thank you Lawrence, Jamie, Chad, Darren, Neil, Ken, Dave and Rand.

A thank you to my medical team who have helped me through my multiple injuries. My specialist Dr. Dhawan – one of the nicest men I have ever had the privilege of meeting. My genius physiotherapist, Dan Bos. My psychologist, Lindsey Jack. My family physician, Dr. Street. Thank you for your support, patience, and expertise.

A special thank you to my representative, Paul Petrie. You have been a saint through my difficulties surrounding the advocacy of my case. Your help and encouragement have kept me going, and your kindness is immeasurable.

I want to thank Karen McGregor, for mentoring me and inspiring me to share my message through speaking.

Thanks to all of our friends, leaders, and members in the Connect Now Network, including Linda and Gord Berti,

i

Caryn and Ed Zimmerman, Warren Schatz, and many more. You are all so special, loving, and supportive.

There are so many other people in the community that have embraced me and my story, providing me with prayers and encouragement throughout my journey. I want to thank Marvin and Shelley Declare at the Psalm 23 Transition Society, you are wonderful people who unconditionally give to others. Thanks to Coach Denis Kelly and my whole football family at W.J. Mouat, as well as the Abbotsford Falcons, which includes fellow coaches, parents and players. You gave me a safe place to grow and volunteer through my recovery. You all mean so much to me.

I send my gratitude to all my Instructors, the Business and Disability departments, and all of my fellow students who have kept in touch with me at the University of the Fraser Valley. Your help, support, and interaction has had a positive impact on my life and this project.

Also, thanks to the family members who have given their support, understanding, and prayers. Especially my sister-in-law Angela, and my older brother Rod; I love you.

Thank you to Nicole Miller for taking the time to look over my book and offering your feedback. A big thank you Kristin van Vloten for your creative edit. Your insights and writing brought everything together where I needed it the most.

To my extended family, the Dunkley's. Your love and acceptance over the years has meant so much, and the way you handled your own trauma was motivating to me. You have always treated me like a part of your wonderful family, and most of my fondest memories involve you. Thank you!

To all my wonderful friends who I grew up with in the Langley community who have kept in touch, you know who you are. This includes, Dan Pool, Mike Witt, and so many others from youth group. Thank you for your much appreciated support, Love you!

FORWARD

Miracle in a Mill is a remarkable story of one person's journey of recovery from a catastrophic accident and a complex set of debilitating injuries to, not just survival, but to a renewed life engagement. It is a journey filled with anguish, fraught with medical missteps and complicated by bureaucratic trap doors. Paul Henczel's honest and compelling story has lessons for us all.

First and foremost Paul has a message for other workers who sustain serious injuries at work. He shares his struggle with unrelenting pain, his battle with opioid addiction and the terrors of PTSD. He does not pull punches. And he does not embellish the impacts. As his representative, I have had privileged access to his medical records, and I can say without hesitation that this book underplays the anguish caused by his injuries. He distills from this sometimes horrendous ordeal insights for other workers to help them not only cope, but overcome their own challenges.

Paul's story is also instructive for professional care givers who provide services to injured and disabled workers. It is especially illuminating how actions by what he calls the "insurance company" can unwittingly undermine recovery, and sometimes do so willfully. His book also underplays the impact that the insurance company's penchant for denial has on his own recovery process. Practitioners who deal with patients with multiple disabilities will gain insight in how the isolated treatment of only one condition without an appreciation of the impact on other conditions can affect recovery.

Miracle in a Mill also has a poignant message for family and support persons and how their sacrifices can make the difference between surviving and thriving. That lesson is perhaps at the heart of this story. Paul Henczel has shared an intimate recounting of his personal journey with all the doubts that attend recovery from a near death experience.

His response to those challenges inspires each of us to ask ourselves some questions. Questions about our own abilities, our limitations, and our response to injury and disablement in ourselves and others.

As the representative for his claim before the insurance company, I have gotten to know Paul Henczel over the last few years. I agreed to take on his case pro bono because he is one of the most highly motivated individuals for his own rehabilitation and recovery from a combination of severe injuries I have encountered in my 40 years working in the Workers Compensation system.

Prior to his 2010 injury that nearly took his life, he was a highly functioning individual in the sawmill industry who had advanced quickly through the ranks to foreman with the goal of working in human resources in that industry. He had already completed a 2 year post-secondary business diploma in 2003 with a 3.5 grade point average.

The sawmill accident that crushed his upper body and stopped his breathing for a pro-longed period left him with a permanent traumatic brain injury and a significant cognitive disorder. Because the accident happened in slow motion, he has been left with a serious post-traumatic stress disorder. He also suffered a number of other permanent physical injuries and is awaiting surgery for a major shoulder injury.

He has been left with a profound complex of impairments that significantly compromise his physical and mental abilities. His symptoms are sometimes debilitating and he re-quires ongoing specialist treatments to manage these symptoms. This is further complicated by a severe cedar allergy that prevents him from returning to the sawmill industry.

Notwithstanding these impairments, He embarked on a journey to complete the last two years of a business administration degree with financial support from the insurance company and sensitive accommodation of his impairments by the University. It was through a determined struggle that Paul has managed to compile a very commendable 3.43 grade point average while completing his degree on a part-time basis. This gentleman's perseverance and commitment to his rehabilitation goals have been extraordinary. He has managed this remarkable achievement while having to navigate a complex, legalistic and somewhat adversarial appeal process to gain full and fair recognition of the extent of his many impairments. With strong support from his treating physicians, he has won his five appeals. His own integrity and his total commitment to maximizing his recovery has been instrumental to this success.

Although the tragic 2010 accident has robbed Paul of some of his abilities, he has re-trained his pre-injury capacity to analyze complex problems and identify workable solutions, albeit at a reduced pace. He has a special knack for absorbing detailed information while at the same time maintaining an understanding of the larger picture. He can see both the trees and the forest.

My career in the worker's compensation system has involved numerous roles. Initially as a vocational rehabilitation consultant, subsequently as a worker's advocate, eventually as deputy chief appeal commissioner with the Workers Compensation Appeal Division, and most recently as a vice chair with the Workers Compensation Appeal Tribunal before retirement in 2013. I have never encountered a disabled worker with the extent of complex impairments Paul Henczel has endured who is also so totally committed to his own recovery and rehabilitation.

Paul Henczel is a very remarkable individual who has much to offer society by his example. His story illustrates that even the most formidable obstacles can be overcome with perseverance, commitment, hard work and support. Paul will make a significant contribution to our society in the years ahead. *Miracle in a Mill* is just the first installment in that contribution.

1

Crushed Alive

"You may not control all the events that happen to you, but you can decide not to be reduced by them."
Maya Angelou

I was being crushed.

Like in a terrible dream, I tried to scream but I wasn't sure if any sound passed through my lips. All I could hear was the crunch and gurgle of my bones and flesh being compressed beneath thousands of pounds of wood. The pressure in my head was so intense I wondered if it was on the verge of exploding.

Is this how I'm going to die? I wondered. *Is this it?*

6 hours earlier...

February 9, 2010 was going to be a special day for my family. It was my son Nathan's 16th birthday. I was excited for the workday to end, so that my wife Jennifer and I could celebrate with him. We had 16 surprise gifts for him to open and we were going to make him his favourite dinner later on.

I ate a quick breakfast, and then made my way along the half hour commute from Abbotsford to Langley, in British Columbia.

I was a supervisor at a large local sawmill. My responsibilities were to manage about 45 employees and to make sure that everything ran as smoothly as possible. The company did custom sawmill cutting. Every order was specific and different, and some were more difficult than others. Sawmill work is not for everyone; it is physically demanding, and the environment also has its challenges. My job paid well which made it a more sought-after position. Although supervising was far better than the other mill jobs, it was still labor-intensive at times. But ultimately, I enjoyed the challenge. That made the time pass by quickly.

February 9th was an extremely busy day. There was added pressure because we were to start cutting for a new customer. We call it a "changeover" when during the shift one order is finished and a new order is started. We were always expected to do this quickly with very little delay. Changeovers inevitably add more work and stress to the supervisor.

The new order started about three hours into my shift. It was a production cut, not a grade cut. In other words, we had to cut these logs as fast as humanly possible. The sawyer that day—the person who cuts the logs—was one of the fastest I have ever seen, and I had to ensure everyone kept up to his pace. I also wanted the customer to have a good first experience, so I was running around more than usual to ensure everyone was on the same page. Every decision had to be made quickly, without hesitation. I made my rounds through the inside of the mill, and then went outside to continue my process.

There is a place where the larger wood - too heavy to pile by hand - comes out of the mill. This is made up of a conveyor-type system of chains, called a timber deck. The wood gets moved onto one of three racks, separated by length, so that the forklifts can take them away.

On an order like the one we were processing that day, the timber deck happens to be the busiest part of the mill. There were three extra people working in this area that day just so we could keep up with production.

On that day, we were cutting a special order of large high-grade hemlock logs. Hemlock is a very dense type of wood that is twice as heavy as other softwoods like cedar and pine. We hardly ever cut orders that primarily consist of large heavy chunks of wood. Most of the wood that day was cut to the maximum size that particular mill could produce for export: 14 inches thick, 21 inches wide, in lengths between 8-22 feet. Those heavy large pieces of wood are called cants in the lumber industry.

CANT - A cant is a very large, very heavy chunk of wood. Imagine a round log with some of the round parts cut off to make a rectangle, and then cut in half. Basically, a cant is like half of a large tree.

While walking past this area, I noticed one cant

3

on edge, jammed against the large steel I-beam that holds up the middle level of the timber deck. At least 12-16 large logs were jammed in behind this one piece, while the chains continued to move underneath the wood. The cant was creating a solid massive wall of wood that would stop production in the mill, and cause downtime if it wasn't fixed right away. These cants were 8–12 feet long, weighing approximately 700-1200 pounds each, or about 100 pounds per lineal foot.

I called for the main forklift driver to come over and assist me. We tried using a forklift to un-jam the piece while the chains were briefly stopped. Nothing was working.

Looks like we have no choice but to manually free this piece up, I thought, aware of how fast the clock was ticking.

I decided to push back the wall of cants that were jammed against the I-beam with a forklift. I figured it would create enough room for two people, one on each end, to rock the jammed cant until it fell on its face. I disconnected the electrical knife switches at that time to ensure the chains would remain stopped. I then had the forklift driver push the cants back as far as he could to give us enough room. I signaled up to the mill, where the cants were being cut to length, to stop cutting.

I asked the individual helping me, while making eye contact, to double check if the power to these chains was still off. They were all still in the down and "off" position, meaning the chains were not moving. The proper procedure would have been for me to put a lock on the switches, and re-check the on switch, which is called being "locked out." Sadly, I did what a lot of people do when they are in a hurry and under pressure to minimize downtime and protect profit margins.

I took a short cut.

I bent my upper body 90 degrees and stepped over one of the chains and under the I-beam. I was in a confined space, only 19 inches between the chain and beam.

In this tight space, my back was pressed up against the steel beam while my entire upper body was bent forward. There just wasn't enough room to sit up straight. I had to straddle a chain with my right leg while my left leg was between the wood and another beam on ground level. There was only approximately eight inches of room between my chest and the wall of wood, which had been pushed back with the forklift earlier. My upper body was twisted to my left so that I could reach the end of the log with both hands. It was uncomfortable and awkward.

The other worker and I then rocked this huge cant until it gained enough momentum and fell onto its face. This occurred between approximately 10:46 and 10:48 am. A foreman is responsible for downtime, and has to record everything to the minute. Right before I crawled into this space, I had checked the time on my cell-phone, which clearly said 10:45 am. And in that two-minute timeframe, immediately after the cant fell, something horrific happened.

The chains started moving. Someone must have flipped the switches up to the "on" position, which immediately initiated the motion detector, firing up the chains. The chains moved quickly, about as fast as a person can walk.

A massive wall of wood slammed into me. I was being crushed against the steel beam, and there was absolutely nothing I could do. I was as helpless as an infant. My mind went blank with terror.

I was being crushed by thousands of pounds of wood.

You've got to be kidding me, my mind screamed. I tried to physically scream, but like in a dream, I didn't know if anything came out. According to witnesses I was indeed able to let out one scream— the most horrific sound they had ever heard. At that point, all I could hear was my body gurgling, cracking, and crunching.

It felt like my bones were breaking. *If these chains don't stop now I am going to die,* I thought, *and I am literally going to be ripped into two pieces!* The opening was too small—how was my body going to stop thousands of pounds of wood from tearing me through this space?

I knew I only had seconds to live. *Someone turn off the chains immediately,* I pleaded silently. *My life depends on it!* I felt like every bit of life was being squeezed out of me. There was so much pressure in my head I literally thought it was going to explode.

Is this my last moment? Am I going to die like this?!
I blacked out.

This is a picture of me and my son Nathan, taken the day before the accident. Nathan was there for his safety training, as he was to start his employment at my mill.

A timber deck. The wood displayed in this picture is typical for what the timber deck normally handles.

This is an example of what a cant looks like. The cants that crushed me were 14 inches thick, 21 inches wide, and between 8 – 12 feet long. The weight is approximately 100 pounds per foot.

PAUL HENCZEL

2

My Fight for Life

"Miracles come in moments. Be ready and willing."
Wayne Dyer

Witnesses said I was out for a long time, between nine to twelve minutes. My employer immediately called 9-1-1. They ordered police, fire-rescue, ambulance, and a medivac helicopter to come to my aid. I certainly could do nothing for myself. My body was squished and contorted between and around the 14 inch wall of wood and the giant steel I-beam.

My co-workers jumped into action. They did not have time to think, just act. They had to move each of these extremely heavy cants off of me one by one, inch by inch, in this tight awkward space. Starting from the far end of the chain and working their way back towards me, two people worked at the wood with picaroon axes.

The man that pushed the last three logs off of me did it very quickly. These were the longest and heaviest logs on the chains. It was an adrenaline-fueled feat of strength that can't be explained with reason. He is a large gentleman, probably around six-foot-five, and approximately 260 pounds in weight. But he should not have been able to push over 3,000 pounds like it was made of foam.

Later, the descriptions received from witnesses explained how my body was miss-shaped. My head, neck, throat, back, chest, right shoulder, and arm were crushed. My entire body was folded, twisted, and contorted in ways that a body is not supposed to move. Some witnesses reported that they thought I was dead. Numerous people said it was the most horrifying thing they had ever seen.

The space I was trapped in was only 19 inches, leaving only 5 inches for my head and upper body. The hardhat I was wearing broke under the pressure. That same pressure also shot my custom-fit earplugs out of my ears.

I was bleeding extensively through my eyes, nose, mouth, and left ear. There was an actual pool of blood on the first piece of wood. It takes a lot of blood to soak into a fresh cut log that has been floating in the river.

When my rescuers finally freed me from the wood, they discovered I was not breathing. But right before they were about to perform CPR, I miraculously regained consciousness. I was extremely disorientated, and in the most severe pain imaginable. It took a few moments, but I began to recall a few things, like where I was and the fact that I had been crushed. I had no idea how I survived.

I thought my chest and back were shattered. The pain was overwhelming. I could barely breathe. Each time I tried, extreme pain would shoot through my chest and throughout my entire body. I tried with everything in me to not panic and to just focus on taking one breath at a time. It was unbelievably difficult.

Then I remembered that it was my son's birthday. *I was supposed to make him pierogis for dinner,* I thought, guiltily. I began to cry.

I could hear people talking and moving. I blurrily registered a tremendous amount of activity taking place around me. I could not see anything clearly because my glasses had been knocked off.

"You are going to be okay," I heard my supervisor say. "Help is coming."

The main safety superintendent at the mill panicked and was unable to respond properly. Someone else had to take control of the situation.

"Where do you feel the most pain?" said the first aid attendant who took over. And, "can you move your fingers."

Speech seemed beyond me but I wiggled my fingers weakly.

"Good! Can you wiggle your toes?"

I struggled for a few moments but then…*yes,* my toes could move. *I'm not paralyzed!* I thought, with the first flash of an emotion other than horror.

The first aid attendant continued speaking to me, keeping me calm. It was an extraordinary feat, given the circumstances. I began to speak weakly,

13

answering the first aid attendant's questions with difficulty. The effort of speaking only added to the pain. My neck and throat were so sore, and my airways felt like they were closing up tighter and tighter with each passing second.

The first aid attendant asked me if I had pain in my head and neck. I had no idea I had been bleeding out of every opening in my head. I had no idea that my head was crushed. The fact that I could hardly breathe worried me, so that's what I focused on. Everything was confusing and disorientating, but I knew to do whatever I could to just breathe. I knew I had to have an inner will to survive.

Eventually, the paramedics arrived and put a brace around my neck. It felt like my neck was being crushed all over again. I had to fight for every breath of air.

Breathe in, breathe out, I instructed myself. *Breathe in, breathe out.*

I was choosing to live.

The first aid attendant and paramedics could not find a consistent pulse on my arms or neck. It beat sporadically. I had low blood pressure, rapid-shallow breathing, cold-clammy skin, dizziness, and weakness— signs that I was going into shock, which can be as life threatening as the incident that I had just endured.

I was confused by everyone's reactions. I was confused by their confusion. The rush of activity around me was overwhelming. I just knew I was conscious and that I had to fight with everything inside of me to stay that way.

The paramedics loaded me into an ambulance. I would have gone by medivac helicopter if I had been less responsive, and today I wish that was the case. I could feel every vibration and bump from the ambulance radiating torturously throughout my entire body. Every little bump made it more difficult for me to breathe.

During the ride there was a lot of confusion and worry because the paramedics could not find a proper line and pulse. On my right side, there was no pulse at all, and it was sporadic on my left. *Just try to breathe and stay awake,* I urged myself. The paramedics talked back and forth, trying to figure out how to manage my situation. It wasn't comforting, but it did increase my curiosity. Listening to this confusion might have made it easier for me to stay awake.

The ride seemed to take forever. The torch relay for the 2010 Vancouver Winter Olympics was taking place that day in New Westminster, where the hospital was. The ambulance horn sounded constantly once we were off the freeway.

When we finally arrived at the hospital, I asked a paramedic if she could honestly tell me what she thought was wrong with me.

"Without a shadow of a doubt," she said, gravely, "your clavicle is shattered, you have multiple fractured ribs, and your lung is collapsed. I have no idea about your neck and back until they give you a CT, but we're mainly concerned about your organs."

My organs! Her words frightened me. *What is wrong with my organs?*

I definitely was not out of the woods yet.

In the trauma area of the hospital, many doctors and nurses surrounded me. I heard at least eight different voices and a lot of commotion. I hurt more than I thought was humanly possible. They performed many tests and gave me a long CT scan, which just added to my pain. They raised my arms over my head for part of the scan, which felt absolutely horrible. I wanted to scream, but I had no energy. I wanted to give up. Everything was so unbearable.

Something has to change, I thought. *I literally can't take it anymore. This fight has to be coming to an end.* With horror, I realized how close death was and how helpless I was to resist it.

But then… I was touched by an angel.

"It's not the events of our lives that shape us, but our beliefs as to what those events mean."
Tony Robbins

A drawing of the space I crawled into, and the position I was sitting in before I was crushed.

A drawing based on witness statements and my injuries, of how my body was crushed and pinned. The distance between beam and chain is 19 inches... the wood took up 14 inches of that space.

*A picture of the piece of wood my blood soaked into,
taken immediately after the accident.*

3
Miraculous Survival

"When we amplify the best within us, we can achieve something miraculous."
Brendon Burchard

It was Jennifer. My wife arrived at the moment when I needed her the most.

She could only recognize my hip at first. My face and body were too miss-shaped, bloody, and severely bruised to register as belonging to me.

"Can I touch him?" she said, the trauma thick in her voice. Someone must have nodded, because she caressed my shoulder and head ever so slightly.

I love you, I thought. *I love you and the kids so much.*

Feeling her at my side, I started to believe things would be alright again. I had some fight left inside of me after all.

The paramedics and trauma doctors spoke to my wife and I separately. They told us that, without a shadow of a doubt, my clavicle was shattered, I had many broken and crushed ribs, my right lung was collapsed, my Adam's apple was crushed, and I had cartilage and ligaments torn in my neck around my thyroid. They needed to wait for the results of my CT scan to comment further on my other injuries. They kept stressing their concern for my organs. I was monitored every 10 minutes around the clock for potentially life threatening Sepsis, which is body-wide inflammation resulting from trauma. I was moved from the trauma unit to a critical care bed.

It seemed to take a while to get the results from my CT scan. When the first doctor came in he started reading from his report, saying that my Adam's apple had been crushed. I placed my left hand on my Adam's apple, because I could not move my right side.

"What exactly does that mean?" I said.

He stared at me in amazement and said, in a shocked voice, "You should not be able to talk at all."

He told me I should try to keep my head and neck still and then abruptly left, without mentioning the other injuries listed on his report.

It took a long time for the doctor to return to report what else was wrong with me. There seemed to be some confusion between the doctors about the extent of my injuries. Certain reports did not match what other doctors told Jennifer and I. There were, and still are, many unanswered questions.

Meanwhile, our kids made arrangements to come to the hospital. My daughter Ashleigh asked someone to drive them to the hospital, because she knew they were both too upset to drive. When they heard what had happened, they didn't understand how I was alive. While Nathan waited at school to be picked up, his friends tried to comfort him by praying for me.

When I saw Ashleigh and Nathan appear in my hospital room, I felt a surge of joy, a little boost. But the worry in their eyes broke my heart. I felt guilty, but at the same time it motivated me. I did not want anyone to have to come see me like that day after day. Nathan tried so hard not to show his distress to me, but I could see that he was worried, horrified, and traumatized.

A number of other people came and visited me that night, including my sister-in-law, Angela, which cheered me up. A few came from my mill because they wanted to see with their own eyes that I had actually survived. They were literally in shock that I was alive and responsive. Apparently, when the ambulance left the accident scene at the mill, they did not turn on the siren right away, leading everyone to think I must have died.

It definitely helped to see how so many people cared. It helped me to take my mind off of my bleak situation, even if it was just for a moment. I remembered the loneliness I felt before my family and friends arrived. Family members heard nurses whispering amongst themselves about how amazing it was that I was alive.

"I can't believe he doesn't need a tube to breathe," they said. "And how is he talking?"

I had a fantastic nurse that first night, which brought some calm to Jennifer and I. It relieved us to know I was in good care. She came promptly when I called, and if it was not time for my next round of meds, she would calmly and reassuringly explain she would be back. She always kept her promises, which helped, and she always had something nice to say. It honestly felt as if she was an angel. Reassured by her presence, Jennifer went home to be with the kids. We agreed that would be best even though she wanted to stay with me.

The pain was excruciating that first night. All I could do was hope the next round of painkillers were coming soon. I had hallucinations all night, maybe from all the medications I had to be on. I was scared and traumatized, and had no idea what was happening at times. Every tiny movement and breath caused a lot of discomfort. The pain came in waves.

I wished my wife was still there to comfort me. I did not want to go to sleep. *What if I do and I never wake up?*

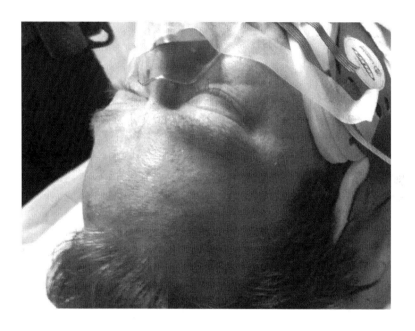

This picture was taken later in the day after my wife had wiped all the blood off my face. You cannot tell in this black and white picture, but the petechiae on my face was more severe.

"No matter how small you start, start something that matters."
Brendon Burchard

4

Sit Up, Stand Up, and Walk

"The greatest accomplishment is not in never falling, but in rising again after you fall."
Vince Lombardi

Early the next morning, Jennifer couldn't sleep. At 4:00 am she started a Facebook group asking for any additional thoughts and prayer. Soon, I had hundreds of people sending us their best wishes and prayers. Their love and support reached me, carrying me through the darkness and pain.

When Jennifer arrived at the hospital, she was immediately surprised to see me looking a bit better.

"Your chest!" she said. "It's taken back some of its old shape!" The severe bruising still rendered me unrecognizable, but Jennifer didn't hesitate to encourage me. It was so good to see her. After the night I'd had, her company was comforting.

My nurse that morning was horrible. She was the exact opposite of my angel from the previous night. It took so long to get my meds, hours after I was due for more. When I asked her for them, the nurse got mad.

"I'm having a bad day!" she snapped, "You're bothering me."

"Well," I said, in as nice a tone as I could muster, "however bad your day is going, mine is worse. Can you please bring the meds you promised me?"

Shortly after that, the nurse had to take my blood and change my IV bag. She forcefully grabbed and pulled my arm. She dropped a needle on the dirty floor, and then used it on me anyway. She yelled at me and Jennifer, who took pictures and a video on her cell phone, incredulous over what was happening.

My sheets had still not been changed. They were covered in sawdust from the accident, which made things more uncomfortable. I am sure they did not want to move me the previous day as they had cut off all my clothes, and I was hooked up to so many machines. But when Jennifer mentioned the sawdust, I could feel that my skin was itchy and irritated. She definitely thought clean sheets would be a good idea, but how was I going to be moved?

There were some doubts and concerns about when I would be able to move around and walk again. But I was determined.

With no help from the new morning nurse, I decided to try sitting up on my own. It took a few moments, but with a lot of struggle I was able to sit up and eventually stand. I was pretty excited I could do that despite the overwhelming pain. I decided to try to walk and go to the bathroom on my own since my catheter had been removed.

It took a while, but I walked ever so slowly. It was extremely painful, and after about 10 yards or so I did not think I could do anymore. It felt like a truck had hit me. Every step shot pain up my whole spine, making me just want to lie down again. Jennifer asked for a wheel chair to get me back to my bed, because I felt like collapsing. The nurse refused, pushing me further. Upset and angry, I struggled back to my bed. We had to complain to one of the head managers after all of that in order to get another nurse.

On a brighter note, I also had a few other visitors that day. A dear family friend named Warren Schatz came by to listen, offer his support, and pray. He was a tremendous comfort.

After how I had been treated that morning, we decided that I would probably get better care if I went home. I remembered how worried Nathan had looked the night before, and how he was putting off his birthday celebration until later, and I just wanted to go home to him. Looking back, it was maybe not the best choice. I should have been transferred to the Abbotsford hospital. I was glad to be going home, but I could still barely move.

Before returning home I wanted to get to a mirror. I wanted to see what others were seeing and how bad I actually looked. When I had visitors, I could see the worry and horror in their eyes when

PAUL HENCZEL

they first saw me, and I knew I must not have looked too good.

With Jennifer's help, I made it to the bathroom and stood in front of the mirror. I was horrified by what I saw. I look like a monster, I thought, observing the deep bruising and the blood that filled my eyes. I started to cry. I have never seen anything like this before, not even on TV. Jennifer tried to relax and comfort me.

"Will you still love me?" I said. I felt like a Beast to her Beauty.

When I left the bathroom, I saw one of my doctors in the hallway.

"Am I going to look like this for the rest of my life?" I said.

"No," he said. "It could take a few months, but it should start to go away after that."

It seemed to take forever to get to the front of the hospital, even with help. While I was waiting for Jennifer to get the car, I thought about how surreal everything felt. It was hard to process everything that had happened over the last 28 hours. I was pretty loaded up with pain medication and feeling disorientated. But I was happy for my second chance.

As we pulled out of the parking lot, I called Nathan to tell him we were coming home. His voice had a cautious tone, but he also sounded optimistic and joyful. The car ride home wasn't fun for me, only slightly less painful than my ambulance ride.

But it was glorious to be home, especially since

there had been a few moments over the past day when I didn't think I would make it there.

Immediately after I arrived, I needed to lie down. That's how I spent most of the next days and weeks: lying down. I could not go up the stairs, and most of my time was spent in our recliner. I still could barely hold up my own neck and move my right arm. I couldn't grip with my right hand. I was still finding it hard to breathe. Every movement hurt!

I soon discovered that I had to learn the most basic tasks all over again. My list of injuries and complications lengthened after certain symptoms revealed additional problems. My brain injury symptoms were persisting every day and my right shoulder was a mess. My voice had permanently changed, my neck and back were not getting any better, and I was always scared.

I was slowly finding out that recovering from my multiple injuries would be a huge challenge every day. I had been in good shape before my accident. I rarely got sick, never broke a bone in my body, and had a lot of energy. Initially, I thought that if I could survive and walk away from that horrific accident, I might only need a few months to recover. Boy, was I ever wrong.

At home, all I could do on my own at first was go to the bathroom. Mind you, that task was still difficult. I could handle getting help for everything else, but I had to do that one thing at least. I pushed myself because I thought it would be humiliating if someone had to help me wipe myself.

I told myself, *Do what you can until you can do more.* I had to push through the pain to get to the point of at least taking care of myself.

I had a home nurse for the first few weeks of my recovery because Jennifer had to go back to work. My nurse helped me with all the things I could not do on my own. I could not even bend over to put on my socks, and literally every tiny movement I made would send waves of pain throughout my body. While she was with me, I was so grateful for my home nurse. But then my insurance company took her away—seemingly for no reason. I was forced to do more, and I did not think I had much of a choice. All I knew was that I did not want to be a major burden. I was a man who had his physicality taken away and I had to fight to regain some of it.

I started by trying to do some personal hygiene tasks and putting pre-made meals on a plate. I was then able to progress to doing some simple household chores. It was like I was starting over, having to re-teach myself almost everything. There were times when the slightest movement would cause severe spasms in my back and neck. They would radiate up into my head, and the only thing I could do was lay down and ride it out, screaming in pain. Sometimes those spasms would take an hour or more to go away.

It took more than a month before I could stand with my back to the showerhead, even with low water pressure. I would have people wait just outside the bathroom in case I fell over. I had to try little things, and at times the results were not positive. I would remember the time I got up and walked in the hospital, telling myself, *"You can at least try."* I told myself the same thing again and again.

Sleeping was nearly impossible. I would usually pass out for a few hours at night when the pain was more severe. Every morning I forced myself to get out of bed, and those initial struggles helped me later on. I began to see that if I could do those little things in an attempt to progress, then I would be able to handle the long and tedious recovery process without slipping into depression. I was so happy to be alive, and thankful for my second chance.

Although I was improving bit by bit, it was hard on Jennifer to not have any additional help. But regardless of what she was going through, she was a constant source of motivation for me. She was strong, patient, and caring. She would take me for walks, and nudge me when I did not feel like getting up. Those walks started out small, and gradually got longer over time.

The most difficult thing to deal with was constantly being pushed around by the horrible bureaucracy of my insurance company. My medical practitioners were ignored. My injuries were neglected and not investigated. Recovery was hard enough without having to fight for everything else along the way.

I was pushed into physiotherapy too soon, made to do exercises that someone with my injuries shouldn't do. No one knew the full extent of my injuries—including me. I was taking pain meds just to get through those visits. It took months to see any progress, as I had no strength or endurance. Any time my heart rate would increase, my migraines and post-concussive symptoms would follow immediately. At times it was like taking one step forward and two steps back. After complaining about my headaches and insisting on seeing a neurologist, I was taken out of physio and sent to Vancouver for a complete neuropsychological assessment.

After two days of testing, I developed the most severe migraine. It lasted most of three weeks without letting up. I was bedridden in a dark room that whole time, suffering. Yet my symptoms and complaints were still being ignored.

I was forced to attend what I was told was a head-injury assessment center over the next three weeks. My insurance company decided to take me away from my family and put me up in a hotel. While I was there they lied to me, refusing to give me the promised medical treatment. Everything I reported went ignored. Unfortunately, I was being manipulated, which only made my complicated situation worse. It was one of the most traumatic and unfair experiences I had to face after my accident.

I was pushed into more programs like that, with the constant threat of being cut off from my injury benefits. My medical practitioners' recommendations again went ignored. I suffered through it all, as promised medical treatments were ultimately refused. On one occasion I was forced into activity in the middle of winter and I contracted severe pneumonia. All I could do was use the suffering as fuel to press on.

Gradually, I was realizing that my overall situation was worse than I had originally thought. My recovery was slow and tedious, my medications stopped giving me relief from my pain, and my migraines were worsening. I was also being told that some of my injuries could be permanent. I was finding it harder to stay positive, and my emotions were slipping. My health and future depended on my ability to fight. The problem was I was running out of steam. I thought things would be getting easier, not harder. I was working so hard, without seeing many results.

I thought that my accident might be a catalyst in bringing my family together. Unfortunately, my parents and siblings were not supportive, which only made the situation worse. The exception was my older brother Rod, who flew up from California, and my sister-in-law Angela. Their support meant a lot to me during that difficult time.

Another blessing that helped in that difficult early recovery process was the hundreds of people who would stop by to visit. Kids I used to coach football would pop by during and after school. Parents and coaches I knew from football came by to cheer me up. Also, people from my work and other friends from the community wanted to see how I was doing. They had all heard stories about my accident and wanted to see me with their own eyes. Their love, best wishes, and support were comforting. They all helped in giving me a little happiness, which would serve as a reminder to stay positive when things got rough again.

Sometimes Jennifer and I talked about how I probably should have stayed in the hospital. The fact was, I made a difficult decision based on limited information. I choose to look at the moment I chose to leave the hospital as my first silver lining. Some people believe the will to live is ingrained in us, while there are others who would call it instinctive. I had that will to move on and get back to my safe place. I had that will to live again. I could not control everything that had happened to me, so I had to make the decision to not be reduced by my circumstances. That will to live was what compelled me to leave the hospital. And in the bigger picture, I knew I was better off having had that will inside of me, driving me on through a complicated recovery.

There came a point where... Against all odds, I made a decision. I made a choice and my long process to acceptance and recovery had begun.

First, I had to sit up, then stand up, and then walk!

In the coming chapters you will see that this was a theme throughout my recovery. For every challenge that arose, I would start by doing what was necessary, then what was possible, which led me to achieve the impossible.

Me and my beautiful wife taken three-and-a-half years after my accident.

PAUL HENCZEL

5

A Different Perspective

"It is support that sustains us on the journey we've started."
Marci Shimoff

Obviously, I was not the only person who was impacted by the accident. Most of all, my wife and children suffered alongside me. So at this point, it makes sense to let them describe their experience of my accident.

Jennifer's Experience

I was at work when Paul's boss called me at about 11:00 am and told me that Paul had had a crushing accident.

"What does that mean?" I said.

"Well, he can move his fingers and toes, so that's a good sign. You should go to the hospital right away. Do you want a taxi?" His tone of voice was kind but deathly serious, so I said, "No, I'm leaving right now."

With a 45-minute drive ahead of me, I told

myself to just concentrate on driving safely. I prayed. It took all that I had to stay focused.

A few blocks from the hospital, worry tried to creep in and I said out loud, "There's no way I'm going to lose my best friend today!"

As I got closer to the hospital, I was re-routed because the Olympic flame was coming through New Westminster that day.

I didn't know my way around very well, and before I knew it I was miles away from the hospital. I asked someone for directions, but they sent me the wrong way. The streets were filled with people and cars watching the flame go by, and I just kept getting farther away from the destination I so desperately wanted to reach.

Finally, I found my way to the hospital. After some parking frustrations, I made my way to the emergency desk, and asked for Paul.

"He's not here," the receptionist said. "There's nobody by that name in emergency or anywhere else in the hospital."

I was stunned. "Can you please double-check?" I pleaded.

"Well, I'm quite sure he's not here, but ok."

I bent over, saying, "This is not happening! This is not happening!"

From behind the desk, a man said, "Who are you looking for?"

"Paul Henczel! He was in a crushing accident."

"He's just around the corner," the man said.

I rushed around the corner into the trauma unit.

At first, I couldn't find Paul because I didn't recognize him. Then I saw his hip, and I thought it must be pretty serious because they had taken all his clothes off.

Are they prepping him for surgery or something? I wondered. There was a great deal of activity—doctors, nurses, and machines—all around him. I approached cautiously, awed by the gruesomeness of what I was seeing and thinking someone was surely going to stop me from walking right up to him. But they let me through.

I was overwhelmed at what I saw. Paul's eyes were clenched and it was obvious he was in immense pain. His face was covered in blood, which I could see had poured out of his eyes, nose, mouth, and ears. His head was purple and red with bruises. He looked smashed up everywhere. His chest was visibly caved in and looked broken and crushed. I had never seen injuries like that before. It felt like time had stopped and the air had been sucked out of the room.

When I knew he could be touched, I brushed his shoulder and head with my fingers and said, "Paul, I'm here now. I'm with you."

I was stunned to hear him speaking, telling me how much he loved the kids and me. He was alive. I was thrilled.

Looking at his chest, I asked the practitioner standing beside me, "What is wrong with him?"

"For sure he has a broken clavicle and multiple broken ribs," she said, "but we're not sure how many and which ones yet. We're also checking on what is wrong with his head."

The critical care doctors monitored him and took tests regularly throughout the day. His eyes remained bright red from being continually filled up with blood.

I kept asking if the blood could be washed off his face, but no one would help me. They were focused on more important things. After a few hours, I found a cloth and a sink and I washed off all the blood, all the while thinking, how could anyone survive this with all this blood pouring out of their head?

The initial reports had not been good. The hospital staff were still testing and monitoring him regularly for organ failure and other things. I just kept thinking over and over again, I'm just so glad my husband is alive!

A kind police officer arrived to investigate the accident, interviewing both of us. Paul was able to slowly give her an account from his perspective. She took a lot of pictures and suggested to me that I also take pictures with my phone.

Everything was spinning. I was trying to stay calm. I was taking everything in mentally, but I wonder now if I should have taken more photos and notes.

I was very comforted when my children arrived. I could see the relief in their eyes when they talked to Paul and saw that he was okay for the moment. Everyone was uncertain as to what was going to happen to him, but the kids and I were just glad to see that he survived.

The next morning when I saw Paul, it seemed like something supernatural had happened. Although he was still in poor condition, he looked so much better, with his chest no longer totally caved in. I thought, "What am I seeing?" It was not just a subtle change. He had undergone a dramatic change from the night before and I was in awe.

Paul and I didn't get all the information about his injuries and condition upfront, which added to the discomfort of the situation. There were three investigations: one by the police, one by the mill, and one by the government. It took a number of days, then weeks, and then months to get a fuller picture of the incident and his injuries. For example, we didn't know that Paul's head had actually been crushed until a few days later. It took more than three years for Paul to get an MRI on his shoulder where we found out that his shoulder had been badly torn up by the accident. His shoulder was left undiagnosed and without treatment for that time, causing further damage.

Initially, after we returned home, we had dozens of people visiting Paul. He would be too modest to say this, but Paul is an outstanding husband and father, and he is well liked in the community. Through sports coaching and announcing he has inspired many young people. In the coming weeks, we estimated far over a hundred people passed through our house.

For several weeks after the accident I was beyond exhausted. But I had to go back to work almost right away, and I could hardly keep myself upright. I had trouble doing anything, and we didn't have much help, but the emotional support from those who rallied around Paul was very meaningful to us.

It is difficult to ask for help, isn't it? When things like this happen, you really find out who your real friends and allies are.

I was so touched by how unexpected parts of the community showed caring towards Paul that I wanted to create something similar for entrepreneurs. I was a part time entrepreneur at that time, while working at a job. I got most of my clients through networking, so I invited some people to lunch to see if we could support each other in our businesses. I had 50 business owners show up that day. This showed me that there was a real need for a place where entrepreneurs could support each other. I started a membership and one chapter, and I'm so thankful for many of those initial attendees who became founding members and friends. I found support in the community among my fellow entrepreneurs.

I now have 14 chapters throughout my province, and the network is still growing. I'm expanding across the country and North America now. Sometimes we have to create the solution we need.

Now I am a full-time entrepreneur. I have successfully created a community of reciprocity and collaboration, where business owners can find support from one another. It continues to take courage, efforts, energy and time beyond my means, but I'm doing it. All because we chose to see the positive side of our situation.

Paul is an inspiration to me each day. We love and support each other through every challenge. We're overcoming what appear to be impossible barriers every day, and creating opportunities for ourselves and others as we go.

Ashleigh's Experience

"Dad has been in a work accident. We don't know how bad it is."

The words were on repeat in my mind as I waited for my brother Nathan to get out of school so we could go to the hospital. My mom had phoned me in the morning to tell me that dad had been crushed, but he was able to move his toes and fingers. I didn't know what to think, or whether I should think at all. Her words just kept circling in my mind.

When 2:30 pm rolled around, my eyes were puffy and I was trying to get a hold of my brother. When I finally did, I told him to call mom. Shortly after that, I called back to make sure he was ok and that he had someone with him until I got there to pick him up.

My friend drove Nathan and I out to the hospital and back. It was such a relief to see that my dad was awake and able to move his arms and neck.

Being with him that afternoon and night definitely gave me peace of mind. I knew that he was going to be ok, regardless of how long it took.

The next day, Nathan and I planned to visit my dad in the hospital again, but I hadn't heard anything from my mom for a while. I was about to call her when suddenly she and my dad walked through our front door! We were so surprised; we hadn't expected to see our dad home for a while, let alone walking by himself.

My dad's survival and quick healing was such a miracle. His recovery continues to be amazing.

Nathan's Experience

When I first heard about the accident at about 3 pm on February 9th (my birthday), I thought my dad was in the hospital for something small like a broken finger or a minor back injury. My sister gave me the news calmly—probably so I wouldn't get worried. I was waiting for my mom to call back, but I wasn't too anxious because I had a feeling everything would be ok.

When my mom finally had time to call me and tell me briefly what happened based on the information she had at the time, I was in disbelief. I didn't understand how he was alive. The situation was much worse than I expected. Tears started to come out of my eyes even though I still knew everything would be fine. While I was waiting for my sister to pick me up and bring me to the hospital, my friends were there with me, comforting me.

Together, we prayed for my dad.

The drive to the hospital was very quiet. My mind raced with the different possibilities of what could happen to my dad. I was trying to imagine how this could happen. I only had a very general idea of what had happened so I did not know what to expect when I saw him.

When I stepped into dad's room, a giant load of suspense and anxiety lifted off of my shoulders. I knew he would be alright.

The first hour in the hospital was confusing and overwhelming. Seeing his eyes fill up with blood frightened me. However, I was certain my dad was in good hands when I left to go to bed at home. I decided that going to school would be the best thing for me the next day. I would get encouragement from my friends and also hopefully get my mind off of it. I did not feel bad about forgetting about it at certain parts of the day because I had a feeling that I shouldn't worry.

One month after the accident, I started working at the exact same lumber mill my dad did. Ultimately, I worked there for over three years in various positions. For the remainder of high school I was on the clean-up crew. This position had me climbing in and through tight spaces much like the one my dad had been in. I was thoroughly taught how to follow "lock out" procedures and I took it upon myself to stay disciplined in the protocol. Because of my dad's accident, I never crawled into a conveyer, a saw, or any kind of machinery without first following the proper safety steps.

During this time, people at the mill took any chance they could to ask about my dad. Some genuinely cared for him and some were condescending and obviously did not understand the severity of his injuries. A few times people would even say that they thought he was "milking it", suggesting that he was fine and just enjoying his time off.

In the summer of 2012, I started working full time at the mill with some of the same crew members that my dad had supervised. The questions escalated from there, until there were basically no questions left to ask. Most of my answers were vague and unsatisfying to my coworkers, mainly because I was unclear about my dad's state as well. All I knew at the time was that my dad was constantly in pain, had multiple injuries, and that it was unknown as to whether he would ever work at the lumber mill again, but that he was taking the necessary steps to improve his condition.

Today, I no longer work at the lumber mill, but I still tell people about my dad's accident, and the most common response I get is a loving and empathy filled one.

Our amazing children, Ashleigh and Nathan.
Ashleigh is a men's wardrobe consultant and loves cats.
Nathan is a Real estate agent and loves adventures.

PAUL HENCZEL

6

Wounded, but Not Finished

"Circumstances do not make a man, they reveal him."
Wayne Dyer

It is my hope that if you are going through difficult challenges this book will help you to find the courage to move past the discomfort and embrace your new life. To have perseverance and determination to overcome whatever obstacles are holding you back.

For me, those obstacles are my multiple injuries and how their complications have affected me both physically and mentally. I want to talk about some of my remaining physical and cognitive injuries in this chapter, and then share what I have done to manage my situation.

I know the struggle of overcoming what appear to be insurmountable challenges. I understand now what so many people deal with on a day-to-day basis. Physical and emotional pain can affect every area of your life. At times my obstacles seem endless and that can wear on me. It is hard to believe that I am still fighting to recover from my injuries more than six years after my accident.

I suffer from multiple traumatic injuries that complicate each other to various degrees. Each part of your body relies on everything around it to function properly. When one area is injured the surrounding parts will be negatively affected as the body naturally tries to compensate. Compare it to your car: every part of the engine has to be in proper working order or the vehicle will break down.

The first time I tried shaving after my accident, my entire right side went numb and gave out, causing me to fall over. It felt like my body forgot that it had feet underneath it. I could not even pick up a glass of water without feeling like I was being electrocuted. I had to learn and suffer through the most basic tasks, until my body got used to doing that activity again. It was hard because when I moved too suddenly I got dizzy and nauseous. My head always hurt.

Anoxic Brain Injury

Ultimately, my most serious injury was my anoxic brain injury. Adequate oxygen is of course vital for the brain. When oxygen levels are significantly low for four minutes or longer, brain cells begin to die. After five minutes, permanent anoxic brain injury can occur. My insurance company has always attempted to minimize the time I was unconscious without oxygen, ignoring the facts. In my case, and according to the initial witness, accident, and first-responder reports, I was unconscious, with a lack of oxygen for between nine to twelve minutes.

This means I regularly suffer from debilitating migraines and headaches, which can last for days or sometimes weeks. I have at least four or five severe migraines per week, plus a constant dull ache in the back of my head and neck. There is a steady ringing in my ears, and my eyes often feel like they are sinking further into my head. My brain hurts, which naturally makes me more irritable and emotional. At times I am restless and do not feel like myself. I have such a variety of headaches and migraines that vary in intensity and length. They are inconsistent and hard to pinpoint. My short-term memory is slippery and some of my long-term memory has disappeared completely. Reading is still difficult for me, especially if it is online.

I can wake up with headaches, low energy, and feelings of sleep deprivation. I can't process things clearly because I am in a constant brain fog. When I wake up with my brain hurting, it negatively affects everything. I feel overwhelmed and frustrated and my day hasn't even started.

I experience all of this despite doing everything I can to take care of myself. I exercise, have a healthy diet, and take all the vitamins and supplements recommended to me. But everything I do is a chore. This, unfortunately, is my inescapable reality most days.

I have learned that a brain injury interferes with the way the brain normally works. Information cannot be sent in a normal way to each nerve cell. My body and brain are not getting the proper signals to function properly.

Imagine having a bad concussion that never goes away.

One of the problems with mild traumatic brain injuries like mine is that the symptoms can be long lasting if not treated in the acute stage. The actual nerve cell bodies themselves are acutely vulnerable to damage and that damage can be irreparable when left untreated. Unfortunately, my nervous system never had the appropriate time to heal and recover. Until I found the right physiotherapist, my entire nervous system was being stressed. My body was out of whack and displaced through my spine in four different spots. In the words of Dan Bos, my physiotherapist, and a specialist in concussions:

The crucial part of post-concussion rehab is to allow the nervous system to become stressed gradually and slowly. If activity is progressed too quickly, symptoms return and the central nervous system becomes stressed and goes through an irritable phase before it returns to an optimal functioning level. If the nervous system is stressed too frequently, there is a chance that full neurological recovery may not be possible. (Bos, 2014)

I have had to figure out over time how to appropriately pace myself after experiencing the numerous drastic results of being pushed beyond my capacity too early. This was by the insurance company case manager and staff medical advisors who never once examined me. This continues to be a learning process for me as I look for new ways to help manage and cope with my chronic brain injury symptoms.

Dealing with the chronic effects of a brain injury means that I also had to fight an emotional battle. I had to move past hopelessness. I did not ever want to slip down the road to depression, so I had to fight through those feelings. Some of those times were better than others, but it was frustrating when things did not move along as I hoped they would.

Too many people get trapped into that downward cycle of depression and hopelessness. Some of them don't have enough support. Some battle the addiction of opiates. Some struggle with an overwhelming feeling of failure.

Every three months I receive anywhere from 70-90 Botox and Facet-block injections. These are injected into the most stiff and inflamed muscles all around my head, neck, spine, and shoulder. These help in bringing down the overall intensity and duration of some of my headaches and migraines. They do not eliminate my symptoms entirely, but they do help me to manage better. I believe I would not be able to function nearly as well if I did not receive these injections. It hurts a lot in the moment when I receive them, but it is actually a fairly quick process. It can take a couple weeks for them to settle down, and the effects wear off a week or so before I am scheduled to have more. This means that they work, so ongoing treatments are recommended.

It took three years to find the right specialist to administer those injections. Dr. Dhawan (who practices in Vancouver) recommended my dosage be doubled and expanded them to include my neck and spine. This has turned out to be way more helpful than the injections that were previously administered by the specialist who was appointed by my insurance company.

I enjoy sports. Since my accident I have been more intrigued than ever with concussion analysis and what others go through. Recently, I read an article about an athlete who was diagnosed with a concussion. He talked about how frightening it was to be in a brain fog and to not feel like himself. It was incredibly frustrating for him because he was not able to do anything about those symptoms. He had his symptoms for just four days. I could completely relate to his frustration.

Most concussions result from a blow to the head, whereas my brain injury resulted from a lack of oxygen to my brain for a significant period of time. The mechanism of my injury forced blood and pressure into my head as I was being crushed.

With the added emphasis today on concussion research in sports, I can only imagine the consequences a team would face if they ignored those symptoms in an athlete. But apparently when the sufferer in question is an injured worker, it doesn't matter nearly as much. At least to the insurance company that exercises control over the medical treatment.

I intend to learn more about the brain and brain injuries to hopefully answer some of my numerous questions. Research has not yet caught up, but I will wait for the breakthrough that could possibly aid in my recovery from my chronic brain injury symptoms. The following are some of my main symptoms.

Sleep Disorder

Before my accident I never had an issue with my sleep in any way. I could fall asleep anywhere, anytime, and quickly. Now, it is one of my biggest struggles.

As a result of my brain injury and complications from my Post-Traumatic Stress Disorder, I now have a significant sleeping disorder. This includes moderate to severe sleep apnea, significant insomnia, and restless leg syndrome. Test results showed I would stop breathing more than a hundred times a night, sometimes for more than 90 seconds at a time. For the first two years after my accident, I averaged only one to three hours of sleep per night. The few times that I was able to dream, I had horrific nightmares and flashbacks. I woke up not knowing where I was and feeling afraid to fall back asleep. Reliving and experiencing my worst horrors all over again in vivid detail is extremely unpleasant and disturbing.

I went through sleep therapy sessions for the first two years after the accident. This helped me to realize how patterns affect my sleep. I kept a detailed sleep diary to identify any negative patterns so I could try to correct them. It was a tedious yet necessary process.

I choose to look at aspects of my sleeping disorder as a blessing in disguise, because I believe I would have had way more flashbacks if I'd dreamt more. Ultimately, it took more than five years to actually fall into much-needed REM sleep, and dream on a regular basis.

Cognitive Disorder

I have had two comprehensive neuropsychological assessments done. The first one was in June 2010, and the second one was in July 2014. The 2010 neuropsychological testing established measurable impairments in attention, speed of mental processing, and memory.

My insurance company case manager concluded in April 2013, that the cognitive disorder had healed. The insurance company refused to carry out further neuropsychological testing, although this was recommended by three different practitioners. I was finally able to gain acceptance of my cognitive disorder through the appeal system. This, with the help of a thorough neuropsychological assessment and excellent medical legal opinion from one of the top neuropsychologists in British Columbia.

The following is part of the conclusion from Dr.

Schmidt's comprehensive neuropsychological assessment and medical legal opinion, dated October 20, 2014:

I would conclude that this disorder is most likely multifactorial in nature, and contributing factors quite likely include anoxic brain injury, ongoing pain problems, problems with sleep and fatigue, and symptoms arising from Post-Traumatic Stress Disorder, although it is impossible to put a relative weight on those various factors. What is more important, however, is that despite the passage of time and treatment of all the problems that underlie, his Cognitive Disorder persists. Hence, it is my opinion that the likelihood of further improvement in his emotional, cognitive, and behavioural difficulties is quite remote.

It is my opinion that the Cognitive Disorder-NOS and the Post-Traumatic Stress Disorder will have an ongoing and significant impact on Mr. Henczel's ability to function adaptively in his life and, in particular, to pursue his academic goals. It remains to be seen just how successful he will ultimately be in this regard and, more particularly, whether, when and under what circumstances he will be able to return to some sort of gainful, competitive employment.

Having a cognitive disorder has made learning difficult. There are times I lose part or all of what I have learned, and some tasks take longer to accomplish. There are other times I get frustrated and irritated with myself when I try to recall things or when I have no idea what someone is talking about. That can lead to some negative thoughts like, "Wow, do I feel stupid!" Or: "They really looked at me like I am crazy."

People who don't know me cannot "see" my cognitive impairment, which can be frustrating as well. I had to work through those negative thoughts, which was not easy. I have had to remind myself that just because I have cognitive problems does not mean I am less intelligent.

Another example of a learning difficulty is math. I used to be quite good at math. I had an aptitude and patience for those types of problems. Now, my tolerance is drastically lower and my focus is a problem. Numbers and equations tend to blur together now and my headaches start immediately when I concentrate on problems.

Most of the time I meet my frustrations with acceptance and the understanding that other parts of my brain still work well. I can recognize when I have to take a break, or when something is useless to fight through. Pacing myself is the most important thing I can do, as to not aggravate things further. Unfortunately, I have had to learn the hard way through trial and error. Letting go and realizing that I don't have to fight through everything has been important. When I was able to see that, I found my learning increased.

Right Shoulder
Some of the worst pain I have ever felt came in

the emergency room right before my CT exam. When the doctors had to raise both of my arms over my head, it made my right shoulder feel like it was being ripped from its socket. From that moment, I knew I had a problem with my shoulder. I had no strength whatsoever in my right arm and could not lift it overhead.

The specialist appointed by the insurance didn't focus much on my shoulder and neck problems. On May 2, 2012, I paid for an independent medical examination by Dr. Steven Helper, which documented atrophy of my right para-spinal muscles. Dr. Helper indicated in his report that I demonstrated:

...gross abnormalities of the right shoulder complex. He has abnormal posture, movement and strength of his right shoulder girdle. He likely has ongoing, incompletely treated, soft tissue mediated pain from the right shoulder complex.

However, in July 2012 the insurance company case manager and staff medical advisors concluded that my shoulder injury had healed.

Unfortunately, it took close to four years to obtain the recommended MRI of my right shoulder. That MRI revealed tears to my rotator-cuff and labrum tendons, and tendinosis in two of my other tendons. Having being involved in football most of my life, I am quite familiar with those injuries. Every athlete who injures those areas usually receives surgery immediately.

The insurance company medical advisors concluded that my documented shoulder lesions were the result of the aging process. Not due to the thousands of pounds of wood pushing against my right shoulder, forcing me into the 19 inch opening.

It took over 18 months in the appeal process and a compelling medical-legal opinion from my specialist Dr. Dhawan, to gain acceptance of the documented shoulder lesions that were due to my workplace injury. That whole appeal process started near the end of 2014.

Although my insurance company finally acknowledges my shoulder injuries, I am currently still awaiting approval for surgery. That company's neglect and denial of my injuries has been a complete injustice. It's also caused other complications. I cannot sleep on my right side and if I do happen to accidentally roll over in the night, my entire right side goes numb. Also, if I sit in an armchair with my elbows resting, my right arm will go numb. I have abnormal posture, movement, and strength in my right side because of this injury.

As a result of my shoulder and nerve problems, I have been twice diagnosed with thoracic outlet syndrome. Thoracic outlet syndrome (TOS) is a painful condition resulting from the compression of nerves and blood vessels. Sharp, shooting nerve pain radiates throughout my arm and into my neck, chest, and back. I feel it with even the slightest bend or turn and that makes it hard to reach for things. I suffer from this condition daily which has also impaired my circulation. Just recently I suffered second-degree burns to the knuckles joining my fourth and fifth fingers to the back of my hand. I simply did not feel the pain in time to jerk my hand back.

I have tried to strengthen the muscles around my shoulder to the best of my ability, but my scar tissue in that area makes it difficult. I can do light house chores, but when I make the wrong move I feel sharp pain. I simply cannot do anything using my shoulder muscles without feeling sharp pain. So I try not to lift my arm and extend it out front or to the side. I do not do anything that involves lifting overhead and I avoid exercises where I would push away from my body. I have tried every non-surgical method to improve my shoulder but nothing works.

An independent orthopedic surgeon has carefully evaluated my shoulder injury and documented lesions. He has recommended surgery and indicated that I can get up to 40% improvement in my function with the surgical procedure. This recommendation is supported by my treating specialist Dr. Dhawan, and by Dr. Gurdeep Parhar.

However, the insurance company has been reluctant to approve surgery. They referred the issue of authorizing surgery and TOS back to the same staff medical advisor who gave the opinion in 2013 that my shoulder lesions were due to the aging process. He opposed authorization for surgery under my claim, reasserting his original opinion that the shoulder problem was due to the aging process.

Soft Tissue and Nerves

I sustained severe compression injuries to the soft tissues around my head, neck, chest, lungs, shoulder, and mid-to-upper back. I also injured my brachial plexus. This is the set of nerves that runs from the neck, through the shoulder, and into the arm. In laymen's terms, I experienced temporary paralysis on my right side. I have frequent severe spasms in my right neck, back, and shoulder muscles because of this. These compression and nerve injuries complicate my thoracic outlet syndrome, causing additional problems.

Complex soft tissue damage takes the most time to heal, a lot longer than a broken bone does. Every layer of muscle in my back was crushed, and I had to find a way to bring them back. I had little stabilization and strength left after my accident, and even now I am still struggling with those issues. For example, I cannot swim or tread water because of the lack of support in my mid to lower back. I start to sink almost immediately.

Neck, Throat, and Voice

I suffered a fracture and damage to my thyroid cartilage. My original doctor in the hospital was shocked that I did not require a tracheotomy or airway stent. As a result, now I have voice hoarseness and significant vocal changes. I cannot sing like I used to, as I have completely lost my falsetto range. Sometimes, I can only talk for a short while before I start losing my voice.

Even though my Addams apple was crushed, my insurance company has denied any relationship between my accident and these problems. Unfortunately, I was told an MRI would not show the nerve damage I probably suffered in those areas. I am starting to investigate some ways to rehabilitate my voice, but my other more pressing injuries have taken priority with my practitioners.

Thoracic and Cervical Spine

During my accident, one of the most severe points of impact was to my neck and upper back. I have height loss between my discs, protrusions in my neck indenting the matter surrounding my spinal cord, and artifacts within my spinal canal. These have caused mechanical and strength restrictions and a lot of extra stress to my nervous system.

My insurance company decided in 2012 that my neck injuries had healed. These ongoing neck injuries were eventually accepted through the appeal process in December 2015.

I continuously suffer from significant pain, tightness, and weakness in the major neck and back muscles used to stabilize my spine. There are times when sharp, intense pain will shoot down the length of my spine and into my extremities. I have little strength in my neck as a result. These complications have contributed to some of my severe headaches, when the pain shoots into my head.

Lungs and Chest

I had multiple fractures to my ribs and my clavicle was shattered. My right lung was punctured and collapsed as a result of those fractures. This produced permanent scarring and other complications that go along with that.

I am prone to pneumonia because of the scarring to my lungs, causing me to be hospitalized on two occasions. These injuries have been complicated by a significant work related cedar allergy that has been accepted by my insurance company. This severe red cedar asthma has resulted in a persistent and chronic cough. My lung capacity is greatly reduced as a result, and I need to take two puffers daily. Every air-born irritant can greatly restrict my airways, making it hard to breathe. I do my best to avoid those by using two air purifiers for our home.

My situation is complex. It's difficult to manage. And I have never exaggerated my injuries or symptoms in any way. My treating practitioners have all stated this to some degree. For example, my specialist Dr. Dhawan stated this in his medical legal opinion on January 29, 2015:

> *I would like to mention that Mr. Henczel has come across as a stoic, matter-of-fact individual, very straightforward in his presentation without evidence of any symptom exaggeration behavior. He has cooperated with all investigative and treatment suggestions. His presentation has always been consistent.*

I shared this detailed list of my injuries and their complications in part to illustrate a point. The bottom line is that my body and brain did not have the appropriate amount of time to heal after my accident. My injuries were never investigated or diagnosed properly, and I was pushed into inappropriate activity too early. My injuries turned out to be more numerous, severe, and complicated than anybody initially thought. I had so many symptoms and the more prevalent ones simply took priority over some of the others. This meant that I had to investigate those other, neglected injuries on my own through the years.

All of this made me feel at times like I was in a losing battle.

Most of my injuries are undetectable by the human eye. And some people have a hard time believing what they cannot see. But at least this has taught me not to underestimate what others are going through. I don't judge a book by its cover. And expanding my own awareness has helped me to understand the power of my emotions and the interaction they have with my behavior. I now know exactly how important empathy is.

Empathy helps to let life in so that it can touch you. Imagine if we were as educated about our emotions as we are in using our intellects. Understanding what someone else's condition is through their perspective will open up your whole world. It will make you less alone.

I live with pain every day of my life, but it does

not have to control me. There are bad days where I cannot do very much, but I live for those days when I can do more. It is my long-term goal to have more good days than bad ones. I make it a habit to laugh and to find something I enjoy every day. I have a lot to live for, a reality that came into sharp focus when I regained consciousness. My wife and kids are so dear to me. The key for me is to hold that close, to not take it for granted.

I had to start by looking for those silver linings, for the positives that came from my situation.

7

Painstaking Journey

"The secret of success is learning how to use pain and pleasure instead of having pain and pleasure use you. If you do that, you're in control of your life. If you don't, life controls you."
Tony Robbins

After my accident, I had to be on a lot of prescription drugs to manage the pain from all my injuries. I took approximately 50 pills a day. I was on OxyContin, other pain meds for nerves and muscle spasms, muscle relaxants, anti-inflammatories, and sleeping pills—to just name a few.

I didn't even know what OxyContin was until Jennifer told me about it when I left the hospital. Now knowing what Oxy was and what side effects it can cause, we made the choice to not take it as regularly as prescribed. I took another pain killer consistently while taking Oxy only when things were at their absolute worst.

These medications were necessary at the time and they served their purpose. For months, the pain was so excruciating that all I could do was wait until I could take my next round. It was a painful journey, filled with setbacks and what seemed like minimal gains. It was like I was in a constant fog, so I don't remember a lot of specifics from that time.

Yes, the opiates I took did relieve my pain somewhat. But I had to balance that with the multiple side effects they caused. These included nausea, vomiting, drowsiness, dizziness, itching, dry mouth, irregular heartbeats, confusion, hallucinations, delirium, and constipation. Living with these side effects took a toll on me. Plus, having to take so many drugs was taxing out my liver.

In my case there came a time when my medications ran their course, and stopped giving me any relief. This was about ten to twelve months after the accident. But the meds had started to mess with my mind to the point where I just had to have them, whether they were helping or not.

I was addicted, and did not see or realize the behaviours I was exhibiting as a result. Getting off those meds was extremely hard. I, like many people who get addicted to painkillers, believed I needed more of the drug because my pain was worsening. I did not realize that the worsening was a result of the painkiller use itself.

The ups and downs of my addiction caused harmful physical behaviors. For example, I would overuse an injured part of my body at my physiotherapy sessions. I couldn't even tell what was working at physio and what wasn't. I also had poor posture because of the lack of sensations I had while in positions that should have felt uncomfortable.

It took a while of being off the drugs to correct the bad habits I formed. As many people can attest, withdrawal from medications is extremely unpleasant. It often felt like an intensifying of the very symptoms I was trying to escape from. I experienced pain, digestive problems, and just general feelings of being unwell. As soon as I took the drug again, some of those unpleasant symptoms disappeared. But taking them stopped being an option. It was horrible, but Jennifer would tell me that it would get better, and that what I was going through was normal.

Working at the mill had allowed me to know other people who had accidents and got addicted to prescription drugs as a result. For example, I was the primary witness a few years before my trauma to my co-worker's horrifying accident.

I was waiting in my car before my shift was about to start when my co-worker drove by, saw me, and gave a wave. He was leaning slightly out of his window to get my attention and took his eyes off the road. His car veered to the left, causing him to run into one of the huge front-end loaders we used to move giant piles of sawdust and wood chips. The bucket went through the windshield, almost taking off his head.

I ran without hesitation to this horrific scene. I helped him get out of the vehicle, ripped off my shirt to help put pressure on his massive head wound, and held his head while I told him to stay calm. It was a miracle he survived that accident, but in my opinion, he went back to work too soon. He ended up falling into the downward cycle of habitual prescription drug use, which led to him losing his job years later. It was a tragedy.

The struggles of my co-workers with injuries and prescription drug use were hard to see, but ingrained in my memory. They ultimately motivated me to nip my own drug dependence in the bud. I also made sure to not drink alcohol throughout my recovery. I knew deep down that it would only make things worse in the long run, so I avoided it.

It was extremely difficult to manage my pain for about a year after I got off meds, which was two years after the accident. At times, I never thought it was going to end. I was tempted to go back on pain medications many times. I would think, *they stopped working when I used them for too long, but I bet they would work great now that I haven't been on them for so long.* But I just didn't like the side effects they gave me, and I could see more clearly what those were when I was off the drugs.

Exercise can be a good tool for pain management. When you exercise, the body produces natural chemicals that work to inhibit pain signals to the brain. Unfortunately, I was not able to work closely with my doctor to create a progressive and appropriate exercise program that helped me deal with the pain. Instead, I felt worse because I was pushed too hard by my insurance company who seemed only interested in getting me off benefits. Ultimately, this caused me to re-injure my neck and shoulder in the beginning of 2012, setting my recovery back. I wish I had a better understanding of how the medications worked, and how they affected my body at the time, but I was in pretty deep.

The neck and shoulder injury meant I had to take pain medications again—the same ones I was trying so hard to stay away from. But the pain and muscle spasms were severe and debilitating so I really had no choice. It took five months to get through that setback, and to re-gain the progress I had been making in my recovery.

Ultimately, the pain meds created a hard cycle to break out of. As usual, Jennifer helped me find a way through it. She could see what was going on and cared enough to ask the hard questions, which challenged my thought patterns around the opiates.

Jennifer used to say, "You won't have any idea how you can manage your pain and what you're truly dealing with until you get off the pain meds." She could see they had again run their course, were messing with my mind, and had stopped helping. For a time, I was doing exercises my body was not ready for, because my mind did not know any better. I had to avoid the temptation to take more, fight through the withdrawal symptoms, and listen to what my wife was telling me.

I don't know what I would have done if it wasn't for her. I probably would have ended up like so many others who get addicted to prescription drugs because they can't think straight. I know that I would not be where I am today if I was still on prescription drugs.

Pain is a symptom of a greater problem, and until you get to the root of that you may just be aggravating your symptoms. I personally believe now that proper recovery cannot start until one is completely off of opiates. I understand that they are necessary, useful, and needed for a time. But it's crucial to look for alternatives when they run their course—which they always do at some point.

Unfortunately, there were many days when I thought I was losing my mind. These feelings could not all stem from getting off the drugs. There was something else at work, but I had no idea what was happening and I could not explain what I was feeling. Once again, Jennifer recognized it and tried to bring it up, but I was scared. I was frightened most of the time, and did not know why. But I would soon find out.

8

Battling PTSD

"Don't dwell on what went wrong. Instead, focus on what to do next. Spend your energies on moving forward toward finding the answer."
Denis Waitley

It was the breakthrough I had been waiting for.

I had been seeing a psychologist for a few months. She had started to recognize some clear patterns in my experience. One day, she showed me a complete list of post-traumatic stress disorder (PTSD) symptoms. As I read them, I broke down and cried...*I have every single one of these!* The diagnosis was clear: I had delayed onset post-traumatic stress disorder.

PTSD, for those who don't know, is a mental illness caused by exposure to trauma—specifically, trauma involving death, threat of death, sexual injury, or sexual violence. Episodes like my crushing accident can make you feel "out of control" in a really serious way, and that loss of control can really do a number on your mind.

Living with PTSD is like being emotionally frozen in the moment when you lost that control. The upshot is that you're nearly always feeling stressed out, on edge, despairing, or numb. And sometimes it even feels like you're "re-experiencing" the traumatic event, especially when you come across situations or stimulus that reminds you of it. Picture the troubled war veteran who has "flashbacks"—he/she is the classic example of PTSD.

My PTSD diagnosis reflected the symptoms that taxed my ability to cope with my own accident. At the time, I was also still struggling to get off pain meds, which were messing with my ability to think straight. Also my numerous physical injuries were getting most of the medical attention. All of those complications prevented us from seeing clearly what I was going through on a psychological level.

I had to trust my psychologist with my concerns. I wanted to learn everything I could about PTSD so I would understand what I was dealing with. I had to accept the fact that I would experience many ups and downs in life and that healing would take time. The slow process to acceptance had begun.

I had to tell my family members and friends about my condition. Jennifer was, and still is, my greatest support. I could trust her with everything because she was not judgmental. She was always willing to listen to me, and offered her love and support when I needed it most.

It now made sense to me why I couldn't drive for more than a year after my accident, and why I was frightened to even step foot in a vehicle. For months, I would have to recline my seat and just close my eyes. I always gripped the door handle, hoping we would get to our destination quickly and safely. I would freeze and panic if I heard sirens. I would also have a panic attack when approaching the exit off the freeway that I used to take to go to work.

Jennifer continued taking me for walks. She nudged me when I did not feel like leaving the house. She encouraged me to exercise and that helped me to "burn up" some of my tensions.

I tried to seek out information to help me make sense of what had happened and understand what I could expect. I fought to find treatment and support from people that I trusted. I needed help from people who expected the best for me and were able to accept how I was at any given time.

One PTSD symptom that is hard to deal with is when I get easily startled. When I startle, it's overwhelming and painful, and my whole body tenses up. My nerves are always on edge. Even the slightest noise or movement makes me feel like I am having a heart attack. Constantly being startled is frustrating, but I have found ways to deal with it. I try to make light of it after it happens because most of the time it isn't serious. This helps me get over it quicker.

I experience various types of panic attacks.

Sometimes I wake up with them in a cold sweat. This is frightening and disorienting in those initial moments when I do not know where I am. I also have vivid flashbacks that rocket me right back to the moment during my accident before I blacked out, or moment when I first regained consciousness. Fortunately, those flashbacks started to become less frequent when I recognized they were symptoms of PTSD.

One nightmare I had stands out above all the others. It combined all of my emotions, fears, thoughts, and pain symptoms in the most vivid package. It truly felt like I was re-living my accident all over again, step-by-step. When I woke up I was experiencing the worst panic attack. While crying and shaking, I found it extremely difficult to breathe. I woke up Jennifer, who was understandably scared. She held and comforted me. After a while, she gave me the advice to go back and change the outcome of that dream. It was the perfect advice.

On another occasion, Jennifer and I went to see the movie *Captain Phillips*, about when Somali pirates hijacked an American ship. Near the end of the movie, there is a scene where Phillips (played by Tom Hanks) is completely shell-shocked. He can barely make out what the woman in the infirmary is saying. He slowly tries to remove his shirt as the medical personnel clean the blood off his face. Then, it all seems to hit him at once. Phillips, who remained completely calm and composed throughout his terrifying ordeal, begins to sob. He then starts to convulse and can't stop sobbing. He shows the completely raw vulnerability, shock, and confusion of trauma. It was a well-acted scene with few words; perfectly portraying what going through a traumatic experience feels like. Jennifer and I stayed in the theatre crying for almost a half hour.

I have found out the hard way how difficult PTSD is to manage. It can come up at any given time and literally control you. Plus, my brain injury symptoms would complicate my PTSD and vice versa. I can get irritated, scared, and emotional. There are times I can feel all of those negative emotions at once.

In July 2012, my insurance company concluded that all my physical injuries had healed and that my ongoing problems were due to "a pain disorder" implying that my pain was all in my head. That just made things worse, because I knew that wasn't the case. Furthermore, my practitioners, including my psychologist, knew this was not true. She always reported that everything I was experiencing was symptomatic of my PTSD and my medically documented physical injuries. I could not allow myself to even entertain what I knew was not true.

I was not able to look at wood in the same way after my accident. That meant I had to start the process of re-exposure. Exposure therapy involves exposing yourself to stimulus that makes you anxious until you gradually reduce the anxious feelings. I started by going to Home Depot, and standing next to various sizes of wood until I could move on to larger ones. I had to get over certain wood smells as well, because they could trigger my symptoms. After a while I could look at lumber trucks driving on the road without having panic symptoms.

Then I began re-exposing myself to the mill where I was injured. This was not even possible and effective until I was off my pain medication. At first, Jennifer would drive me when the mill was not running and no one was around. My son had started his weekend cleanup job at the mill, so we would arrive before his shift ended. I would just sit in the car and wait for my panic sensations to go away. We did this for months until I felt comfortable enough to get out and walk around. It was a hard and slow process that required patience.

One day I decided to drive myself to the mill and try it alone. Upon arrival, I had to go to the bathroom so I decided I would use the one at the mill. This bathroom was separate from the main mill, located between the main building and the parking lot. I started to have a horrible panic attack. I thought I was having a heart attack. At the time, I had no idea what was happening so I called Jennifer to tell her how I felt. It took nearly 45 minutes to calm down and relax.

At times I would just shut down emotionally and recluse, avoiding what I didn't know. These were some of my most frightening and confusing moments. Sometimes it seemed like my world was falling apart. Everything seemed black, impossible to understand.

It's hard to explain the feeling of always trying to escape something and never knowing what it is.

Slowly, I began to notice the many things that could trigger my panic symptoms. I recognized feelings that I was not able to put a finger on earlier in my recovery. Back then, I would just shut down and become numb. Jennifer noticed these things and would bring them up in the moment, but I was not able to fully understand what she was saying until I realized for myself what was happening. Not knowing what is happening can make you feel like you are going crazy, which can be lonely and demoralizing.

To this day, I can be watching a TV show or movie that has a trauma scene in it, and it can set off my PTSD symptoms. Earlier on, I was not even able to look at the original hospital reports without having panic attacks. The triggers are never the same and certain things affect me differently than others do. Recently a scene from a movie triggered a series of dreams with flashbacks. These occurred over the course of a few weeks, and would always wake me up in a panic. This negatively affected my sleep in the worst way, setting off severe migraines and headaches that lasted a month. One trigger started a whole downward spiral that negatively affected every area of my life and functioning.

I have to trust that what I have learned will eventually enable me to break out of these cycles and patterns. My process of dealing with PTSD is ongoing.

All I can say is this: don't wait until you break. Learn to cope, then reclaim your life.

I found out through my different channels of support that PTSD had completely taxed out and strained my adrenal glands. This can be debilitating, as your adrenals affect your energy levels and their impairment leads to extreme fatigue. I now take supplements every day to help with this.

I tried to take the time to exercise on my own and eat healthy. I would walk and stretch to help with my mobility. Through trial and error, I found out what foods are best for me. I even started a mostly gluten-free diet, as my wife and daughter are allergic. I notice that I am slightly less bloated and not as fatigued as I used to be. My head is also a little clearer and less foggy. For me, every little bit of improvement helps.

I also improved my mood by not isolating myself. I had to spend time with family and friends and join group activities outside the house. I continued to volunteer by announcing for my son's high school football team. Just doing that for a few hours would knock me out for the rest of the weekend, but I found enjoyment in it. All of these things were therapeutic in their own way. People close to me were motivated by my perseverance, which gave me a boost and increased my confidence.

I found some other activities that also gave me enjoyment. I watched movies and allowed myself to relax and escape into the stories they told. There were some things I naturally felt like doing at the time right after my accident, so I would continue with those while challenging myself in others. This was made easier because of the support from my family, who would give me that gentle push and encouragement I needed.

This particular journey will be an ongoing one for me. Nearly six years later, I am still discovering new triggers and figuring out how they affect my body in different ways. Recently, I figured out that I stiffen up and get panic symptoms when I drive the same route the ambulance took from my work to the hospital. But I look at it as a blessing every time I discover something new, because it feels like a weight is lifted off. This helps me to accept my situation so my mind can move on to the next thing.

Experiencing or witnessing a serious injury can be a life-altering event. It doesn't end with the physical injuries. The psychological fallout can affect your confidence, self-esteem, and even change your personality altogether—and not in a good way. If you've experienced this, find the support you need, and don't be afraid to show some vulnerability. There are people out there who know what you are going through.

It is an unbelievable feeling when you finally start seeing results. Believe me, there were times when I honestly thought that it would not happen. At times I was physically and emotionally out of it, but I pushed past the doubt. I had always heard people, including myself, say that "hard work pays off with persistence." You understand that in a whole new way when you are fighting for your own life. I had to just keep on it, day after day. I would always reflect on that first silver lining I experienced in the hospital, when I sat up, stood up, and walked out. I told myself, *"If you could do that then, you can do this now."*

Many times since my accident my guilt has made me think about my decision to enter that confined space. The fact is, I should have paused and paid more attention to what I was actually doing. I did not appreciate in that moment what the significant consequences of my decision could be. Unfortunately, everyone takes short cuts to some degree in their lives. And it is important to remember that no one is immune from having an accident. Sometimes, taking an extra moment can save your life.

I have gone through different stages of guilt, but the last thing I should do is blame myself. I had to look past the negatives to see the many positives.

Importantly, I began to balance some of my outside expectations with my internal feelings. My reality had changed, and I had to ask myself if I was going to play the same roles I had in the past. I had to come to grips with a lot of my injuries, and accept that I would not be the same person I once was. I had to realize I was given a second chance, and had to determine what that was going to consist of.

When I was fully able to accept what had happened and let go of it, I started to reconcile with my new reality. It was starting to make some sense. I could now continue my new growth, maintain my insight, and focus. That acceptance led to more courage, of which I needed plenty.

I had to draw on what I still had: my wife and kids. Having them beside me through everything keeps me going. I constantly remember the fact that I literally would not be here without them. Their love kept me going. I truly believe it kept me alive during those critical moments.

I have always made the conscious decision to not give up, but instead move forward—even without a lot of answers. It has been incredibly hard, but life is worth fighting for. Rewards do not come easy. Remaining positive helped me to see that things wouldn't always stay the way they were and would have to get better at some point. That would always help me to fight through those feelings of depression.

I had to find ways of coping that worked best for me. These are different for each PTSD sufferer. I had to appreciate those ways of coping and to not give myself a hard time. Having the ongoing support of family and friends helped me to take the opportunity to recuperate. I took time out to relax and also become more active as I was able. I tried to do something enjoyable each day and focus on positive thoughts and memories. I have always tried to tell myself, "Ride it out, tomorrow will be better." Sometimes that particular "better tomorrow" does not come as soon as you would like.

If you suffer from PTSD, don't allow yourself to think there is something wrong with you. PTSD is about what happened to you. I had to personally remember that it is not a sign of weakness to be diagnosed with PTSD. Rather, it is proof of my strength, because I survived!

When something significant like this happens in life, you really find out who your true friends are and where your main circle of support lies. My physical and emotional trauma truly revealed to me who these true friends were. I found out who was there to offer emotional support when my true feelings and vulnerability came out. I needed that unconditional love from my community of support to show me that I mattered.

I could not do it on my own. Nobody can.

9

My Dear Friend

*"A friend who is far away is sometimes much nearer than one
who is at hand."*
Les Brown

I am fortunate to have some close friends who are
there for me unconditionally through everything,
friends I can lean on through the hard times. In
particular, one friend and his family stand out: Ron
Dunkley.

I needed an escape growing up because I did not
feel a true sense of family at home. To make a long
story short, there was a lot of dysfunction in my
family, and I was the scapegoat because I stood up
for myself. Because of that, I tried to surround
myself with genuine people who wanted to get to
know me, for me.

One of the places I would escape to was the
youth group at Christian Life Assembly, a church in
Langley. When I was there, I was able to be me. I
was in a place where people truly accepted and loved

me. I met so many people there. And although we are all grown up now with our own families and do not see each other much, we are still friends. This was where I met the Dunkley family. I quickly grew close with Dean, who was my age, and his younger brother Ron. They became like true brothers and family to me.

The true sense of family I had growing up was at the Dunkley's, my home away from home. From the start, I had the utmost respect for them and believed they were put in my life for a reason. They always made me feel welcome and loved. I felt an overall sense of peace anytime I was in their home. We hung out almost every day, playing sports, or watching movies at their house. Football was our main bond. We all had our favorite teams and healthy rivalries.

Ron was the youngest out of our group of friends, who we called the posse. He looked up to us, but he also brought his own unique energy to the group. When we were a few years older we started going to many NFL, CFL, and NHL sporting events together. Most of the time I would cheer for the away team on purpose just for the fun of it, and Ron found that hilarious. After that we started going to Bellingham every week to buy football and hockey cards. That turned into going to games together locally and down in Seattle, dressing in the away team's gear, and just having fun. You could say we were fans of each other as well.

When Ron was older, he purchased his parents'

home when they moved to Nashville. He worked three jobs, one of which was as a fireman, to pay off his house at a young age. He moved up the ranks very quickly in his firehouse because he was highly respected and had a great work ethic, qualities which he got from his parents. His magnetic and loveable personality also helped.

By this time, I had a family of my own with two kids. Ron understood my new responsibilities, and was always there when I needed him. When my daughter Ashleigh was younger, we went to an NBA game with Ron and some other people. He was so funny, asking what her name was, adding extra phrases to her name, and asking her if he could call her that. She finally said, "My name is just plain Ashleigh, that's what I want to be called." So for years, he called her, "Just Plain Ashleigh."

Ron and I would talk often on the phone. We got together as much as our different lives would permit.

When my son Nathan was older I wanted so badly to take him to an NFL football game. So Ron, his friend Mike from the fire hall, Nathan, and I went to Seattle for a Monday night football game versus the Raiders. On that particular day, and on the days leading up, Seattle was experiencing some of the worst rain and flooding in its history. I had a few Raiders rain ponchos for my son and I, and Mike had his own. Ron whipped out his bright orange Broncos poncho, insisting he would wear it and telling us that it would be futile to try to talk him out of it.

We had a laugh and went to our seats at the very top of the stadium. Imagine in a sea of blue, lime green, and silver and black, one bright orange figure noticeable to all. Every time he would come back to his seat after leaving for the washroom or refreshments, he would scream, at the top of his lungs, "Go Broncos!" Boos would rain down from the crowd, at times drowning out the sounds of the actual game. After a few rounds of inciting the crow, even the Seahawk fans were entertained and laughed. It was one of the funniest things I have ever witnessed in my life.

Ron continued to go on road trips with Mike. He always wanted me to come along, but I just couldn't. They have these adventures in major cities in the US with sports teams. They would plan it where they saw as many sporting events as they could fit in over the course of a few days, sometimes not sleeping much, oftentimes driving from one event to the other over multiple cities. He would call me from some of those trips, which was always entertaining. I believe he made it to every NFL stadium, and about a hundred other sports stadiums, seeing everything from college football to MLB, NHL, and NBA games.

I have hundreds of stories about Ron. The memories are endless. I could write a book about those stories alone. Ron is the funniest, most charismatic and energetic person I have ever met.

After my accident, Ron was one of the first

people to come by to see how I was doing. He was every bit the support I needed, and offered his help any way he could. I could barely move, and he was there just hanging out and making me laugh. He came to the 40th birthday party my wife arranged for me at our house, making that day extra special and memorable.

As a birthday gift, he took me to a playoff hockey game. He drove all the way to my house to pick me up, even though it added an extra 45 minutes each way to his trip. We hung out all night, and he helped me the whole time through my new disability. On the way home I apologized for not being as much fun as usual because of my injuries. He told me, "Henczel, don't be ridiculous. It was one of the fun-nest nights I have ever had." He left that night saying, "I'll always be here for you, bra!" That meant the world to me, knowing I could always count on him in my life.

Unfortunately, a few months later, that would change.

It was late at night, around 11pm, when I heard the bad news. I was on my computer, looking through Facebook, when I came across a message from Dean Dunkley's wife.

She told me Ron had had an accident. The most brutal accident you could imagine.

Ron was hit and dragged for a few hundred yards by a freight train in Seattle. I was confused and horrified; I could not believe this was happening. I called my friend to verify the news and to get more details. It was the true. Ron, at 34 years of age, had sustained some of the most horrific injuries imaginable and was not expected to make it through the night.

I walked downstairs to tell my family, feeling panicked and helpless. Without hesitation, my amazing wife and kids agreed we should all pack immediately and drive down to Seattle to see him. This meant a lot to me, as I was still not able to drive after my accident. That first night, we stayed in a hotel close to the hospital. I did not get any sleep. The images and thoughts going through my head were horrifying. I tried to reminisce on all the good times we had together.

I also thought about Ron's family, the Dunkley's. Their youngest son and brother was now in the fight of his life. I could not imagine the horror they were feeling. Gene and Sandy, Ron's parents, were living in Nashville at the time but they immediately flew down, not knowing what to expect upon their arrival. They stayed by his side, living in the hospital.

I tried to prepare myself for what I was about to see the next morning. I could only imagine what he must be going through, and I knew I needed to be there for him. He had been such a big support for me after my accident; I now had to be that support for him.

Seeing Ron was as hard as I expected it to be. He was unable to talk, highly medicated, and on life support. He would be awake for only a few moments a day. The unbearable pain he was in was evident immediately. Seeing that put my own situation in a greater perspective, and I had to stop feeling as sorry for myself. He was not expected to make it through that first night, yet there he was, miraculously hanging on after forty surgeries. His entire lower body, including his pelvis, was basically torn to shreds. It was one of the most horrific sights I have ever witnessed.

I had just arrived home after visiting Ron again, about six weeks after his accident. Everyone was hopeful and optimistic that he just might make it through. He had taken a lot of strides forward, but he still had a long, long way to go. I was imagining Ron leaving the hospital, and thinking about what it might be like for him at home. It was encouraging to think he just might make it.

That feeling would be short lived.

A few short days after that, I received a phone call. Ron had taken a turn for the worse and was not expected to live much longer. So off I went again, down to Seattle with three close friends. Another traumatizing journey. All we could do was wait.

After an uncomfortable night in the hospital, infection took over Ron's body. We knew his fight was coming to an end. I literally saw it in his face, which had completely changed color.

The doctors were telling the family there was nothing more they could do. At that moment, Ron grabbed my arm, lifted his head, and tried to tell me something. I knew what he was trying to say. It was over. I called for his mom and ran out of the room, crying. Everyone at the hospital gathered and prayed.

A little later, we all gathered by Ron's side as he was taken off of life support. We each said what we wanted to say and sang some of his favourite songs, like "Take Me Out to the Ballgame", and "Amazing Grace".

I watched my friend take his last breath on January 4, 2011, surrounded by family and friends. It was one of the hardest things I have ever done, yet I would not trade that moment for anything.

Ron's body was transported back from Seattle, in a joint effort of the different fire departments. It was touching to see how the first responder community supports and sticks together when one of their own falls. Their precession back from Seattle and across the border was touching and extremely emotional.

Ron had over 1,700 people at his funeral, and I acted as one of the pallbearers. We all wore Denver Broncos jerseys, which would have put a smile on his face. There were two tour buses to transport family and close friends to where he was going to be buried. The police closed the intersections during the funeral precession.

I asked myself many times after his death, *why did I survive? Why me and not Ron?* I didn't have the answer to those questions and it made me feel guilty and confused. Some days I would cry uncontrollably for hours.

I had to figure out my reactions to Ron's loss, and realize it's normal to experience many emotions.

That it was all part of my grieving process. My brain was searching for things that I did not have an answer for, and eventually I let go of the questions.

I told myself, *there is only one way to go from there... up.*

Again I had to make a choice... to overcome or be defeated.

The only thing I could do was to ride it out and fight through those hard times, telling myself it would get better. During this time, I found it was extremely important to take care of myself.

I will always cherish those last two months I had with the Dunkley family and Ron in the hospital. I feel closer to the other members of his family now, which is a blessing to me. Ron's older brother Dean has always been a brother to me, and our friendship is so dear to my heart. Dean, along with his wife Christi and their two kids, give me a tonne of joy. I love them so much. Throughout my recovery, they have listened and offered encouragement.

The way the Dunkley family chose to respond during their time of trauma and loss has been such an inspiration to so many people. They slept in the waiting room every night in the hospital. Through everything they had to deal with, they still found ways to help others. Their faith and hope were instrumental in helping others who were going through difficult times in the hospital. The tragedy brought their family closer.

I have seen first-hand how they have turned their tragedy into an opportunity to help and inspire others. They chose to keep the memory of Ron alive throughout their community by starting the Ron Dunkley Memorial Society; www.rd-ms.com.

Their strength serves as an example to many, and has helped me through my own recovery. Words alone will never do complete justice to what they mean to me.

Ron stood out in his own unique way, leaving positive impressions everywhere. I believe we can all look to this and see a lesson. Find your niche, stand out from the crowd and be remembered. Ron left others wanting more—usually laughter.

Ron, I miss you every day and more than words can say. I still cannot believe you are gone, and wish you were still just a phone call away. Literally, everything in life reminds me of you—it's just weird. To be honest, it sucks and I cry sometimes. I mostly laugh at all the good times, those endless memories and stories we shared together. I wish you were here. Love you, bra!

Ron lived more in his 34 years than most of us will in a lifetime. He would have wanted me to do the same.

*My favorite picture of Ron Dunkley
taken while working as a fireman.*

This picture was taken when Ron's body arrived in Langley, BC, after being transported back from Seattle, WA.

Taken outside of Ron's funeral, which was held at Christian Life Assembly in Langley, BC.

There were over 1700 people at Ron's funeral, with people standing outside. The above picture shows some of the first responders who came from throughout the region, and who are lined up to honor Ron.

Ron's parents, Gene and Sandy Dunkley.
Taken on Ron's memorial bench located outside of his
fire hall, in Langley, BC, Canada.

PAUL HENCZEL

10

Information is Empowering

"Success is peace of mind which is a direct result of self-satisfaction in knowing you did your best to become the best you are capable of becoming."
John Wooden

Information is empowering but many times you have to put effort into finding it.

When I was a few years into my recovery, Jennifer and I paid for a private medical consultation to help find some additional answers. We needed a second opinion that confirmed what my family doctor was reporting, but went ignored.

Although we did not receive all that was promised to us during those consultations, it set the stage to keep investigating my neglected injuries. We decided to do whatever we could to find practitioners who truly wanted to help. We were able to uncover some independent specialists who came highly recommended. We just had to wait for those referrals to go through the medical system.

As if our medical system wasn't already frustrating enough, most doctors do not want to be involved with certain insurance companies for various reasons. Unfortunately, there are not many systems set up to provide injured workers with the answers they need. So once again, persistence was key for me to find answers and start gaining ground.

Out of the blue, right before the summer of 2012, my insurance company gave me their decision. This decision stated that all of my physical injuries had been resolved, despite the overwhelming medical evidence to the contrary. I had officially begun one of my biggest fights.

I was told I had to go back to work or I would be cut off from my benefits. Plus the various jobs they proposed were not at all suitable, given my injuries. My doctors were against this. They had never stated I was able to work in any capacity. How was I supposed to work when the only activity I could handle in a day was light exercise?

I thought that supervising could possibly give me the flexibility and power to manage my situation. If all the physical components were taken out of my old job it just might work. This was a long shot, but I had to give it a try. This meant re-exposing myself to my workplace as part of my therapy for post-traumatic stress. I had to prove I could handle being inside the mill when it was running. It was so hard. I started to avoid some of my feelings and stress symptoms as a way of coping. I would zone out and freeze up, which was hard for Jennifer to witness.

Around this time, I was also seeing some specialists for my various lung issues and chronic cough. One of them proposed I get tested for western red cedar asthma. Red cedar dust is poisonous and can be harmful to your lungs, especially when you are exposed to it as long as I had been. This process took a few months, but near the end of 2012 I was diagnosed with severe red cedar asthma. On top of everything else I had a new health problem to deal with. What was I going to do now?

However, I believe that being diagnosed with red cedar asthma potentially saved my life once again. The damage to my lungs and airways was so bad that being further exposed to the poisonous wood dust on a daily basis could have killed me.

There was no way I could return to my previous employment in any capacity. It was a relief. My re-exposure therapy was too hard and I wasn't coping properly. I was in a constant state of panic, unable to communicate my feelings.

I was also upset to discover that the damage to my throat was permanent, and that my cognitive disorder and brain injury symptoms were persisting every day. The severe migraines and headaches would still last for days, and the pain in my upper body was not getting any better. I had severe right-sided nerve pain shooting through my arm and up into my head. There were times that I could not even pick up a pencil. It was becoming clearer that the gravity of my injuries had been underestimated.

I had to find the best way to pace myself and

PAUL HENCZEL

cope. This meant picking myself up and learning from my failures. I also had to keep finding the missing pieces: the information I lacked. I believe that whatever you are going through, having a thirst to educate yourself can help you find acceptance. When you search with positive intentions, you can sometimes find those pieces you have been searching for and experience great peace. However, understand there might be other times when the facts you uncover unsettle you, so prepare yourself. Ultimately, for me, uncovering my medical mysteries relieved some of my anxiety.

Here are some of the facts and insights I have discovered over the months and years since my accident:

It was determined later in the mills investigation that the chains did not start due to any mechanical issues. Aside from that, there was never a complete and thorough accident investigation by the insurance company's prevention division to determine how the chains were turned on. The two main witnesses both confirmed that the switches were off, and in the down position. There was another witness who said he turned the switches down to stop the chains when he realized I was stuck and being crushed. It would have been impossible for the switches to be up and on while the chains were stopped. This is because there were two sensory photo eyes that, when covered up, initiate the movement of the chains. This was the conflicting piece of the puzzle that was never further investigated.

A few years after my accident, I talked to the police constable who was called to the scene. I wanted to gather up the photos and reports that were taken by her. She could not believe that nobody followed up on how the chains started. She said a few things had definitely stood out to her and raised some red flags at the time of my accident. It was her opinion that someone turned the chains on. But in a workplace accident, the police are no longer involved in the investigation process once the worker survives. It then moves to the insurance company. This is still unsettling to me, but something I can't dwell on moving forward.

The time from when the chains were turned on to when they were turned off was approximately 30-45 seconds, which normally is not considered a long time. However, this was a lot of time to me because I was being crushed. That time frame seemed to take forever, stuck in that hopeless situation between life and death. It is hard to explain in words the feeling when you know that death is near. It is also painful to relive those 30-45 seconds in my head.

I don't remember anything during those nine to twelve minutes after I passed out, thank God. Different people have asked me if I experienced anything during that time, and the simple answer is no. To me, it was like sleeping without dreaming. I am extremely thankful that I was not conscious during that traumatic part of my accident.

These approximate time frames for when I lost consciousness were based on the actual police and ambulance reports, and when first responders were called and arrived at the scene. These corresponded to the witness statements, as well as my later recollection of when the accident actually started. While I was unconsciousness, my head was compressed down by approximately five inches. This is based on the measurements of the space I was crushed into, the size of the wood, and the detailed witness statements of how my body was positioned and wrapped around the cants. Five inches is a considerable difference in the context of the normal circumference of my head. I still wonder how my head did not explode. That enormous pressure to my head did cause severe petechiae, which occurs when there is bleeding under the skin. I found out almost 5 years after my accident that in severe cases it can be life threatening.

I was told later how my co-workers and employers were traumatized the day of my accident. Most of them thought I was going to die. One of the witnesses who helped rescue me explained his thoughts to me in a visit to my house later on. He said that during the 2010 winter Olympics in Vancouver, a luge athlete lost control of his sled. He was thrown off his sled and over the sidewall of the track, striking an unprotected steel support pole near the end of the run. He was travelling at 143.6 km per hour at the moment of impact and died from his injuries. There were pictures of the athlete lying motionless online that my witness saw before they were taken down. He told me that I looked way worse than that athlete. He said seeing me trapped was horrific.

Management sent the crew home for the rest of that day with pay, something that does not typically happen in the lumber industry. I am truly grateful to all those men who helped rescue me from certain death. Their actions gave me a second chance at life. I have only one explanation as to what could have possibly aided in my survival. My right arm and shoulder were crossed in front of my sternum, and took the brunt of the impact and force. I believe if my arm was not crossed in front of my body the way it was, my chest and major organs would have received the direct impact. This probably would have killed me. This is just my opinion, but I believe it makes sense.

When I regained consciousness, my main worry was to just keep breathing. I was not aware of or thinking about the other complications that could have killed me. In my mind, I had just woken up from the worst part, which was the actual crushing. I found out afterwards that people who survive severe multiple traumas can develop sepsis and lose function of their organs. This can also be called "crush syndrome". It's potentially a fatal condition that happens early when people go into shock because their tissues don't receive adequate oxygen. It can also occur later in the recovery process. Apparently, this generally starts with the lungs and kidneys and then moves to the liver and intestines. That's exactly what was happening to me immediately after the accident, and that's what the paramedics and doctors were so worried about.

Those are some examples of information that were revealed over time. We are still learning new facts along the way. It is important to be pro-active in finding the missing pieces.

That day, more than six years ago now, changed my life in so many ways. It was a traumatic moment that put my life on an unpredictable path and forced me to fight for survival.

I believe I have experienced many miracles beyond that initial moment of being crushed. These miracles are not easy to explain. I avoided death, paralysis, and even more severe complications that should have come from the injuries I sustained. No matter what you believe, it is hard to argue my use of the word when you look at its dictionary definition. *Miracle: a surprising and welcome event that is not explicable by natural or scientific laws and is therefore considered to be the work of a divine agency.*

My tragedy has given me a new start, and I am thankful for my second chance at life. I allowed myself to be a prisoner to my own expectations in the past. My accident and recovery have rewritten those expectations. I want to pursue my new life in a bolder way.

Learning is a gift, even though most of the time pain has been my teacher.

"Thinking helps, but intuition will always guide you to the source of love, rather than the source of fear."
Karen McGregor

PAUL HENCZEL

11

Overcoming Adversity

"Our ability to handle life's challenges is a measure of our strength of character."
Les Brown

I wanted to start this chapter by giving you a little background from before my accident that ties into how I started at the lumber mill. It led to some of the things I attempted post-accident.

When I was just out of high school, I started working in the lumber industry. I discovered that if you had your lumber grading tickets, your pay would increase substantially. Lumber grading is when you apply rules to the wood with consideration as to its intended use. These tickets are hard to get and take some people years to achieve. I received all of my "AA" tickets in a year and a half. (You have to get your "A" ticket before writing for your "AA"). I achieved the highest score for a first time writer, and started to instruct and coach those courses after two years.

This led me to the mill I was working for at the time of my accident. I started my employment with that company at the beginning of the year 2000.

Back in 2001, the lumber industry started to decline. The mill where I was working went through one of the worst lay-offs in its history. My employment was not looking promising, and I had a young family to provide for. I decided to go to university to complete my business diploma. My grades from high school were not sufficient, so I had to upgrade my English and Math pre-requisites. I took up to seven courses per semester, which did not include those upgrades. I also worked close to full time hours to help support my family.

It was a huge accomplishment in my life, as I had never thought I would go to university. I was put on the Dean's List and won two scholarships. When I finished, I thought I had the additional skills to switch careers. But I literally applied to over two hundred places without any luck. I was frustrated that my efforts were not being rewarded. I found myself back at the same mill, applying for the same job that I was trying to leave behind. I had to swallow a lot of pride, and try to make the best of it.

I was not happy at the time, but Jennifer told me to hang in there and not give up. She had a feeling something would come up. At least I was well liked and had a good reputation. This made it easier so I continued to work hard. About 10 months after that, I was promoted to the position of junior foreman, in large part due to my business diploma and people skills. My wife was right. I finally caught a break.

I did not have a lot of seniority, which upset some of my co-workers, so I had to work extra hard to gain their respect. It really helped that customers liked and respected me. They trusted me with their high standards in grade and quality, which caught the attention of management. My leadership and people skills helped compensate for my lack of experience. I listened to my fellow employees and tried my best to create an environment where people could put aside their differences and work together. Things were turning around.

The lumber industry was constantly changing so the mill had to start being creative, taking on different and more complicated orders. I proved I could handle the stress in meeting and exceeding the production demands while maintaining quality expectations. These complicated orders were called "matrix" and "temple" cuts. Basically, you could only produce a certain number of pieces according to specific sizes. This can be a challenge and everyone has to be on the same page communication-wise. Producing extra or not enough would drastically cut into profit margins. Certain customers requested that I oversee these quality control aspects. It was challenging, but rewarding knowing the customers were leaving happy.

I enjoyed being a supervisor for the most part and the pay was good. The frustrating part was constantly switching from day shift to night shift. I supervised on night shift, but when things slowed down I was put into a regular production role on a day shift. My wage would also change according to the job I was doing. All of this was hard on my body and my family.

Plus, the mill was not getting any busier so half the time I was doing jobs I did not enjoy. I wanted a change. The problem was that I was getting older and did not feel I had sufficient skills for switching careers. My overall mood was slipping and I was falling further into a rut. It felt like my career choice had trapped me and I had no way to escape.

Fast forward to the beginning of 2013, right after I was forced back into the workforce despite my injuries and then diagnosed with severe red cedar asthma. The despair I felt before my accident was nothing compared to what I was feeling in 2013. I did not know how I was going to dig myself out of this hole, and make something positive out of my life. My battles seemed endless and I did not have the physical or emotional strength. I had to find a way to dig deeper.

I had to make a difficult decision about what my next step would be. I still needed time to recover, and working anywhere didn't seem possible. The other option I had was re-training and going back to school. I had less than two weeks to decide between these two options, both of which seemed unsuitable, given my situation. But choosing neither would have cut off my benefits, forcing my family into bankruptcy while I fought through the appeal process.

In early 2013, I was still unaware of all my complications and limitations, because I was waiting for further diagnoses on other injuries. It had taken years to navigate through the process of finding practitioners who wanted to help me, and investigate the complaints that had gone ignored. I decided to go back to school and attempt to finish a business degree. This meant coming up with a written proposal in less than two weeks in the hopes that my insurance company would accept it.

My proposal was accepted on one condition: I had to take four courses per semester, and two in the summer, I quickly realized that my course load was far too heavy. I was given permission to drop to three courses per semester and one in the summer. I also registered with the disability department at my university in order to take advantage of all the help they could offer. The university accommodated me quite a bit, which helped. But I still had no idea how to manage my course load. I needed tutors for courses that I used to be strong in. My mind seemed like it was failing me.

I found out through the disability department that the province of British Columbia recognizes the maximum course load for anybody with a documented disability is two courses. But injured workers are treated differently. Recommendations from all of my treating specialists as well as the university's disability and business departments went ignored. I was forced to stay in three courses, or else get cut off from my benefits.

On September 22, 2014, my specialist Dr. Dhawan said:

Paul needed to see me today because since last week he has been having daily headaches, neck pain, and migraines. This is making it unbearable for him to get through the day [and] his studies and it is interfering with his sleep and mood. This is unusual because usually he gets two to three months relief after injections. Since he has gone back to school and has an increased course load despite my recommendations against it, he is now having severe setbacks and a decline in his function. This cannot continue as he will not be able to carry on with his educational upgrade. I strongly reiterate what I stated in my previous letters, that he should only take two courses in the fall term, not three... Continuing the current workload not only is counterproductive for his health and functioning but it is not likely to succeed and would be counterproductive to his overall education endeavours. As his treating physician, I strongly urge [his insurance company] to put these changes into effect immediately.

On top of all this, I wanted good grades. Growing up, my family made me feel that I was unintelligent and inadequate. But my wife and past instructors always told me I was smart, so I felt I had something to prove. It was hard to accept that I was not the same person I once was. My accident took away at least half of what I could do before. So I badly wanted to do something that made me feel useful. School did give this feeling to me, but I could not continue at the pace I was going.

Ultimately, Dr. Dhawan was right. My heavy workload had disabling consequences, and almost de-railed my re-training altogether. I was trying to complete something, but at what cost? I needed a break and could not continue fighting every day of my life. I also had to be my own lawyer, because my basic rights were being denied. I was not able to enjoy school or retain a lot of what I was learning.

When I was in the middle of my schooling, I wrote this entry in my journal:

I am having some of the worst sleep since after my accident. The pain in my head and behind my eyes is overwhelming, I can barely keep my eyes open. My migraines are intense and steady all day; all I could do was e-mail my instructor to say I could not come to class. I later went to see my doctor and told him I have had steady migraines for three and a half days with no break.

Most concerning at this point is that I do not even have a time now when the migraines drop in pain to a more manageable headache level. My doctor told me to only do what I can and to not push myself further. He was adamant about that, and told me to just take it easy and understand that I am not like normal people and students, that I am dealing with things most people do not have to deal with. I am fighting a losing battle; I don't think I can do this anymore.

Then, one of the kindest men I have ever met came into my life at just the right time. Paul Petrie was working for the Workers Compensation Appeal Tribunal (WCAT) as a vice chair. We had talked a few times on the phone when I needed assistance with my claim and the various appeal processes. He mentioned how my case was one of the most complicated he had ever seen. He commended me for what I was doing, given the gravity of my situation. That was encouraging to hear when I was feeling defeated.

I gave Paul a phone call some months later. I found out he was retired, which was a little upsetting. He had been so helpful to me with the appeal process, and I needed help again.

Paul invited me for coffee and we got to know each other a little better. I shared the various appeals and difficulties I was involved in and mentioned I was looking for assistance. He ended up giving me the contact information for a colleague of his, hoping he might be able to help me out. Unfortunately, that did not work out.

But the next time we met, Paul volunteered to represent me on a pro-bono basis. Before he came along I was just hanging on. My claim wore on me and he could see that. I was now going to be supported in my ongoing fight with the insurance company. I could cut myself some slack, and realize I didn't have to attain perfection to succeed. I could concentrate on my health and my schooling more, releasing the other hassles to my new representative.

It was an absolute miracle and it came at the perfect time. Paul's expertise and support helped untangle the mess of my complicated claim. I consider him a friend and a saint, one of the smartest and most generous people I have ever met.

With Paul's help, I started to get more injuries diagnosed, some for a second time. Understanding what my complications were and how they affected me in school helped me to realize how to pace myself better. I could not fight through my cognitive disorder and physical symptoms anymore. Since I finally understood that they were permanent, I had to manage and accept what I could do. My practitioners and my wife recommended I take a step back from outside expectations for my own health. I had to let some of the other pieces fall where they may.

There was an economic course I thought for sure I would fail. I could not focus or concentrate on the complicated formulas and material. It was impossible to push myself and every strategy I used did not work. But I miraculously passed that course, maybe due to getting sympathy marks from the instructor. Taking three courses negatively affected my next semester, so I had to decide which course I was going to re-take. My symptoms became so bad that failing one was inevitable. On the last day possible, I was given permission to drop a course.

My insurance company could no longer ignore the cognitive and physical injuries that were becoming accepted on appeals. They also could not neglect the numerous recommendations from my practitioners to have my course load reduced. My training program was finally extended. It had taken a year and a half to win my fight to drop to two courses per semester.

School is hard for any mature and healthy individual. It's twice as hard to overcome with disabilities. I could barely get by on tests because of my short-term memory problems. Trying to focus brought on headaches and migraines. I was so good at math before my accident, but numbers and financials were just a blur. I couldn't spend much time on the computer because of my headaches, torn shoulder, and nerve problems.

I had to compensate for these deficits by relying on my strengths. My maturity and experience helped me to understand what my instructors wanted. I met with them regularly and asked them for help. I am good at writing, so my various reports and projects made up for my test results. There were presentations to give for each project in every class. Public speaking has always been my favourite thing to do, so those skills came in handy as well. I participated in class discussions and did not use my disability as an excuse. I found ways to adapt. I was also strong at organizing my course schedule and balancing the required difficult courses with electives that aligned with my strengths.

I completed my Bachelors of Business Administration Degree with a major in Human Resources. I did it! It was one of the hardest things I did since my accident. I am extremely proud of myself for this accomplishment. The obstacles I had to overcome to succeed have given me the confidence to start the next chapter in my life.

Jennifer and I have always believed in higher education and I value what I have learned. This process has given me much more than a degree and a set of business skills. It helped me to fully realize my limitations and to accept my weaknesses. Much more importantly, it helped me identify what strengths I do have and how I can use those to compensate for my weaknesses.

My university experiences also helped me to develop strong research skills. These enabled me to uncover tools to aid in my ongoing recovery—tools that could be life changing for anybody struggling with injuries and chronic health struggles.

That's what I'd like to share with you now.

*On my graduation day with my friend and representative,
Paul Petrie.*

Friday June 3, 2016. Paul Henczel, BBA!

PAUL HENCZEL

12

Recovery Strategies and Resources

"If you believe it will work out, you'll see opportunities. If you believe it won't you will see obstacles."
Wayne Dyer

If you have experienced a serious injury and are working at overcoming a disability, it may feel as though the world is against you. It may feel like you will never be the old you again.

A disabling injury is among the most challenging experiences you could face in life. Your physical and mental fitness can decrease, causing you to lose confidence in yourself. And if all of that isn't enough, it's difficult for anyone to reliably foretell the path ahead of you. Nobody can tell you what the likelihood of your total recovery is.

In my case, certain things had to take place before others could start happening. First, I had to start developing more patience for my situation. I had to learn to listen to my body and mind when they were giving me signs. Next, I had to stop wallowing in my injury and become more proactive on my road to recovery. When I finally accepted the "new me" and the limitations I had, the improvements followed.

I motivated myself to move forward by focusing on taking baby steps. Later on, when I tackled bigger challenges, I drew upon the motivation I developed in those early stages. Most of the time, I am able to see that what I accomplished in the hospital was probably the hardest thing I have ever done. I try to channel the inner strength I had in those days when times get tough. I always remind myself that hard work pays off. I remain positive and look towards the bigger picture, realizing that there will always be ups and downs.

I believe one of the keys to recovering from an injury is to identify how and where you were injured. You have to identify the root of the problem before you can understand the symptoms. Understanding the effects of your injury leads to greater self-awareness—and ultimately, self-acceptance.

No one wants to experience tragedy. But if you think about it, there are probably many people in your life who have experienced tragedy and emerged from it stronger. Suffering and struggles are a part of life. You can learn from those experiences and move forward when you force yourself to push through, regardless of what shape you are in. Please understand that taking baby steps is still progress. Remember, no one came out of the womb walking and talking.

You can grow more resilient by patiently overcoming your obstacles and tragedies. You can take those valuable skills and lessons and apply them to other areas of your life. There are many people who have created great futures from horrible pasts. You are what you choose to become.

You can learn to face problems head-on, and function in healthy ways. I believe this can be done with a slight shift in your focus and thinking. You can start by looking at your responses to the event, rather than the event itself.

If you have chosen to fight your way through to a glorious recovery, here are a few tips to keep your mind strong and your heart open:

1. **Ask for help:** Find someone you can talk to and trust. You may not be able to do all the things you could before, and asking for help does not make you weak.

2. **Set realistic goals:** Please, set realistic goals for yourself. You have to be able to envision how you are going to get to where you want to be, so "pie in the sky" goals you have no idea how to achieve are not helpful.

3. **Find enjoyment:** Find some enjoyable things you like to do each day. You have to take time for fun and relaxation. This can lift your spirits and help you to look for the positives in your life.

4. **Find professionals who care:** Find professionals who can help you in your recovery

process. This can be hard, but know that there are people out there who genuinely want to help.

I have always looked for any improvements in my recovery, even 5-10% improvements. That percentage may seem small, but when it has to do with the quality of your life it's significant. To secure these 5-10% improvements, I researched various methods online and listened to any suggestion from my medical team to ensure I tried everything. I did not want to leave any stone unturned.

I had to develop my own customized rehabilitation and exercise program. I had to focus on what worked for me, while letting go of the things that didn't. I realized I was the only one who could do this; nobody was going to come around and do it for me. It was not an easy task, as I had to keep in mind all of my various injuries and complications. Most times, I had to resort to trial and error to find what gave me the best results.

The following is a comprehensive list of all the various strategies I have used to help with my numerous symptoms—and perhaps some of these could make a big positive difference in your life. This list also includes various items I have bought to help with comfort as much as possible. My house is set up with the sole purpose of symptom management. Just keep in mind that these are the tools that have proven helpful for me, but everybody's situation is unique. In all things, do your own research and consult with your medical professionals to ensure you're making the best choices for you.

These pain management strategies and tools (in no particular order), include:

1. **Meditation and sleep music:** There is a lot of research out there describing how this is beneficial. Even if you meditate or listen to sleep music just for the purpose of relaxing, it is worth it. The different brain waves that they each target can promote healing in your body, and I personally have a more peaceful sleep when I do it before bed.

2. **Inversion Table:** You can buy an inversion table at Costco for only $200. They help to naturally separate compressed discs and elongate your spine. Two to three minutes a day has saved me thousands of dollars in physiotherapy and chiropractic treatments, while alleviating a lot of pain. I recommend them to everyone I know; it's something anyone with any sort of back pain should own. (Of course, do your research and consult with your doctor prior to trying one out.)

3. **Stretching and Yoga:** This is a must no-matter what you do in life and how healthy you are. Stretching and yoga help to relieve "stuck stress" and folic acid, and correct bad posture.

4. **Foam rollers and the MELT method:** The MELT method is a self-treatment created by connective tissue specialist Sue Hitzmann. It

helps with stuck stress, relieves pain, and promotes a healthier nervous system. It's also something I would recommend to anybody, but especially those dealing with chronic pain or serious injuries. If your doctor believes this method could be helpful, I encourage you to try it out. Here is a link to the MELT website: www.meltmethod.com/about; and a short YouTube video:
www.youtube.com/watch?v=v1Fu-m-MxKE

5. Relaxation and deep tissue massage: Massage greatly reduces muscle and joint pain and flushes your lymph glands. Finding a massage therapist who understands what areas to focus on to give you the most relief is key.

6. Shiatsu: Shiatsu treatments focus on pressure points in your body. Jennifer and I try to do this as often as we can, and it completely re-sets our bodies. You can find Shiatsu practitioners in various public markets or some malls. We personally like the one at Lonsdale Quay in North Vancouver.

7. Physiotherapy: As I mentioned in Chapter 6, I see a physiotherapist named Dan Bos, who is all about helping your nervous system to heal, not just trying to bring you back for more appointments. I would not be where I am today without his expertise. He specializes in manipulative physiotherapy and concussions, which has helped in greatly reducing my chronic symptoms. When it comes to physiotherapy, you need to research what you need, and who is best able to help you though your particular struggles.

8. Acupuncture: Acupuncture has incredible benefits, but again you must research the type that will give you the most benefit. It can be just as easy to find someone who will not help, so ask for recommendations from people you know and trust. In fact, this is a good practice when searching for any medical practitioner.

9. TENS machine: I have two TENS machines, one that we bought from a mall, and one that clinics use for their patients. This machine stimulates your muscles to promote healing, and will pay for itself shortly. It really takes the edge off.

10. Obus-forme back rests and pillows: Over the years, these have improved so much. Research which ones are best suited for you, and figure out which ones you like the most. My sleep and quality of life have improved from using different combinations for my various daily tasks.

11. Certain electric back massagers: There a lot of electric back massagers on the market now, and you just have to try them out to figure out which ones you like the best. Trade shows and malls are great places to test these out.

12. Heat and Ice: Applications of both hot and cold compresses help with inflammation and stiffness. I use both of these almost every day of my life.

13. Peppermint and other essential oils for headaches: Pure natural essential oils can alleviate certain tension headaches and can also be quite relaxing. Talk to your doctor about whether these natural solutions could work for you.

14. Obus-forme mattress tops and head rests: These have helped with my sleep and relaxation. Try the different types to determine whether you prefer softer or firmer varieties. They are also great for supporting your neck and spine.

15. CPAP sleep machine, and sleep therapy, progressing to a sleep apnea dental mouth guard: I went through two years of sleep therapy and four years of using a CPAP machine. The sleep machine helped with my sleep apnea and added oxygen when I slept. But when I started to use a dental mouth guard, I had a more restful and dream-filled sleep. This is going to be different for everyone so use what is best suited for you.

16. A car with an adjustable seat for support: I actually have an older model Toyota, but the seat adjusts every way, which makes driving a little more tolerable.

17. A healthy diet, mostly free of gluten: Every single person's tolerances for certain foods are unique. There is conflicting research out there about diet depending on where you look and the media does not help much. But there are certain blood tests that will tell you which foods your body doesn't process well. They cost a few hundred dollars, but the knowledge you receive is priceless, in my opinion.

18. Games and hobbies: I started playing games and seeking out more hobbies when I found out I had permanent cognitive disorders. They are great for your brain, and they will add some fun to your life. For example, Lumosity is good for your brain and fun at the same time.

19. Natural and organic cleaners and soap: The chemicals in regular cleaners and soaps are harmful to your body. My allergies and the quality of my life have improved since making the switch to natural and organic cleaners and self-care products. I recommend this for everyone, but please research and investigate this for yourself.

20. Natural supplements and vitamins: Most of us are not getting the proper nutrients from the food we eat. I take a good B-12, Vitamin C, liquid Vitamin D, Omega, CoQ-10, Calcium with Magnesium, Serapeptase, Glucosamine and Chondroitin, and a good multi-vitamin. I also take an adrenal supplement, because I found out that PTSD taxes out your adrenals, leading to extreme fatigue. Most women are lacking in this as well, so this is worth your research.

21. Entertainment: Watching sports has always been relaxing to me. It is enjoyable and helps serve as an escape of sorts. Right after my accident, I watched the 2010 Winter Olympics that just so happened to be in our backyard of Vancouver, BC. I also found a lot of joy watching Jimmy Fallon and a lot of movies. Laughing helped me to forget my struggles for a few moments. That has been priceless to me. Everyone has to find what gives then joy in life and gives them a break. I personally gravitated toward certain types of entertainment because of their calming effects.

All of these things in and of themselves are just small separate pieces in the bigger puzzle, but using all of them in conjunction has improved my life measurably. I had to get creative in my recovery, and looking at the bigger picture helped me remain focused on my desired outcome.

The following is a short list of resources I found helpful in my recovery. They have good content and information about either PTSD or Traumatic Brain Injury. The core goals of these services is to help people develop the personal tools to lead meaningful and productive lives. It was vital for me to find information that helped me to overcome the health and medical challenges I was facing. This is true whether you are a patient - like me—or a friend or loved one.

PTSD
www.ptsdassociation.com

www.cmha.ca/mental_health/post-traumatic-stress-disorder/#.V1M0OZErLIU

www.trauma-ptsd.com/en/ressources

TBI

www.societyforcognitiverehab.org/index.php

www.mayoclinic.org

I also found it extremely helpful and motivating to listen to other people's stories about how they overcame their own adverse experiences. Developing a strong positive mindset was key for me to push forward and stay motivated. Here are some of the professionals I had the chance to meet with or listen to along my journey:

Denis Waitley: www.waitley.com

Marci Shimoff: www.happyfornoreason.com

Karen McGregor: www.speakersuccessformula.com

Brendon Burchard: www.brendon.com

Sean Stephenson: www.seanstephenson.com

But beyond any external source of support—any tool or resource—relying on the strengths I developed in my life helped me push past my new weaknesses. Focusing on my strengths helped me to develop a healthier life, and maximize my potential.

And of course there were periods when I had to rely on the strength of others—my family and friends.

If you have been injured or even disabled, what thoughts do you have around your injury? What emotions come up? Try to understand the various sensations you experience, like pain, weakness, numbness, tensing, and spasms. Then experiment with strategies that can help give you some relief.

Experiencing an injury is never fun, but it is not the end of the world. If it was an injury that ended something you enjoy, then find something new. Nobody else can do the work for you. When you take responsibility for your injury and recovery, it will be worth it in the long run.

We all have challenges in life. No matter how bad it seems, there are always silver linings. When we get through the rough times and overcome our obstacles, we should celebrate that we got through them. We need to celebrate our victories. This helps us to recognize what success looks like. So set smaller and bigger goals, because you have the power to make your dreams come true.

If I can manage my issues, others can do the same. Every painful story can have a successful ending.

"There is no scarcity of opportunity to make a living at what you love; there's only a scarcity of resolve to make it happen."
Wayne Dyer

PAUL HENCZEL

13

Crushing Your Cant's

"If you don't know what your passion is, realize that one reason for your existence on earth is to find it."
Oprah Winfrey

I was crushed by cants. But, now I'm crushing my cant's— any obstacles that remain in my way. You see, what my recovery ultimately revealed to me is that I was being crushed by my cant's even before my accident. What were my can'ts? I'll explain with the following statements:

- I can't work in another industry
- I can't get myself out of this rut
- I can't finish my degree
- I can't write a book
- I can't be an entrepreneur
- I can't fulfill my dreams

Those were my can'ts. What are yours?
After a certain point, I could not allow my cant's

to bring me down any further. Since then, it has been a daily choice for me to keep moving forward in my recovery, against all odds. Sometimes it felt like the whole world was against me, but I used that feeling to fuel me. Failure was not an option.

I now try to put the focus on what I can do, rather than what I can't do. I cannot allow myself to get crushed by my emotional can'ts anymore.

As I mentioned earlier in this book, the large pieces of wood I was crushed by are called cants.

Now, I am crushing my cant's!

People have asked me how I stay positive and overcome my challenges. The simple answer is that I divide up my challenges into one manageable step at a time. The first step is sometimes the hardest. When I have a bad day, I tell myself: Just focus on making it through today, and hopefully tomorrow will be better. This is a choice I choose to make, to have hope, to overcome.

After giving it some thought, I have formulated a three-step process for moving from a surviving mindset to a thriving one.

Step 1: Do what is NECESSARY

You have to start somewhere and the first step should be the easiest one. For me, that was breathing again while I slowly progressed through every physical movement. I had to sit up before I could stand up and I couldn't start walking until I managed those first movements. This kick-started the learning process for me.

Learning - through my counselling and schooling, I have learned some important things about how we as human beings grow and progress. For example, in one of my communication courses at university, I was introduced to a model that illustrates the steps in the learning process. According to Robinson and Rose, there are four stages that an individual will most likely go through in the learning and maturing process (Robinson and Rose, 2007). I believe these are the same stages people go through in the recovery process. Thinking about these stages helps me when dealing with, and trying to understand, what I am going through.

1. **Disturbance:** This is when something happens within or around us. An event that will signal that change is necessary. We can often try to explain this away, deny, or ignore it.
2. **Chaos:** This is usually felt as an emotion at first, through anxiety, anger, or becoming tense. You have to respond to chaos by taking control back.
3. **Letting go:** You have to be open to new ideas and possibilities, so that opportunities for something different can emerge. Let go of your ego, and the need to be right.
4. **Learning:** Going from chaos to learning requires courage. Celebrate these small victories, when you move toward a more

complete and healthy process of living. (Robinson and Rose, 2007)

This, for me, is life in a nutshell and the way I choose to grow through it. My disturbance was my accident and my chaos came in the aftermath of that. Chaos is a natural part of learning and it is important to look at it as an opportunity for clarity and change. It takes longer to learn if you follow your first inclination, which is to hang on tighter and dig in deeper, trying to avoid or deny the chaos.

One important and necessary step for me was bringing some order to my complicated injury claim. If you've been injured or know someone who has, you understand how important it is to manage your insurance claim.

You have to start by organizing your paperwork. Paperwork might end up being your main source of discouragement. It can be extremely hard to navigate. It will probably feel like your insurance company or some other entity is just adding insult to injury. This can make you feel overwhelmed and defeated. Rising above that will help you learn and become stronger. You will be left with skills that can help you in other areas of your life.

I had to overcome my fear about the disturbance and chaos of my situation. I have one of the most complicated claims anyone I know has ever had to deal with. My multiple trauma and numerous injuries have created a mountain of paperwork that is difficult to sift through. It was key to separate and organize every medical report and memo into different sections. There is never going to be a right time to do this, but it is important for your own piece of mind and your recovery.

Step 2: Do what is POSSIBLE

When I started by doing and managing what was necessary, I was able to do what was possible. Taking those first initial steps helped me to realize the possibilities. I was able to get off prescription drugs, overcome my friend's death, and manage my PTSD and recovery. I was able to look for the opportunities and stop looking at the obstacles.

I may never be exactly who I was before my accident, either physically or emotionally. But it is important for me to realize that I still am myself. I still matter. It has been a journey of hardships and challenges, but it's up to me whether I wanted to work for my future, or someone else's.

Positive Thinking - This is a mindset strategy that I have always tried to use, even before my accident. I would rather focus on the bright side of life and expect positive results rather than negative outcomes. It is a conscious choice for me to anticipate happiness, health, and success. I choose to believe that I can overcome any obstacle or difficulty that stands in my way.

There are times positive thinking is easier said than done, because many times the answers or outcomes are unknown. I find that by practicing it regularly, positive thinking can become a habit. I do not know where I would be today if I did not employ this strategy.

Positive thinking is contagious. On the other hand, so is negative thinking. It is simple: being negative creates unhappy feelings, moods, and behaviors. When your mind is negative, unhealthy chemicals are released into the blood, which can cause a downward cycle. Frustration, disappointment, and failure are sure to follow. It is no secret that most individuals want to be around positive people, and prefer to avoid the negative ones.

Positive thinking doesn't mean that you ignore everything unpleasant. It just means that you approach those unpleasant situations in a more productive way. You choose to think the best is going to happen, not the worst.

For years, researchers have been exploring the effects of positive thinking and optimism on health. Here are some of the physical and psychological health benefits that positive thinking may provide: ("Positive thinking," 2014)

- Decreased depression
- Lower levels of distress
- Increased immunity to the cold and flu
- Greater emotional and physical well-being
- Reduced risk of death from cardiovascular disease
- Longer life span
- Better coping skills during challenges and

stress
- Higher self-confidence

Here are tips for creating a positive mindset that have worked for me:

1. Being aware of your self-talk: I had to cut myself some slack. I could not put myself down and criticize myself for mistakes. I also had to stop doubting my abilities and expecting failure. When that happens you damage your self-confidence, harm your performance, and paralyze your mental skills. Negative self-talk will cause you to fear the future.

2. Challenge your negative thoughts: Personally, I had to take a long look at myself and ask whether my negative thinking was reasonable. It can be useful to use rational, positive thoughts and affirmations to counter the negative ones. What if we were products of our own decisions, and not of our circumstances? When we choose to react to those circumstances positively, they can actually make us stronger, not weaker.

3. Look for opportunities: Look at your situation and see if there are any opportunities that could come from it. Are there any silver linings? This is exactly what I did. I realized that I was given a second chance at life to do what I always wanted to do. I can't work in the lumber industry or do any physical work anymore, so I

PAUL HENCZEL

created a life of purpose. I had to first apply what I have learned and then implement it into my life. Now I celebrate my renewed confidence!

My passion in life is to help people overcome and transform their own lives. And my accident and recovery have opened up that opportunity for me.

Step 3: Do the IMPOSSIBLE

When you master the necessary and the possible, you will find yourself doing the impossible. I overcame my challenges and completed my Bachelor's Degree. I am also an author and can now use my story to help others. I empowered myself in a way that can inspire and empower others to say "I can", not "I can't."

Story - Telling your story can have a big impact on your recovery. I believe opportunities create stories, and stories create opportunities.

This is what I did. I started telling my own story, and allowing myself to heal and learn along the way. I found out a lot about myself, good and bad. I came to the realization that I wanted to be better, and I allowed myself to find my inspiration.

I have learned that knowing and telling my story has helped me to get unstuck, feel empowered, and inspire others. I believe that when you embrace your story and the true emotion that comes with it, you can overcome those challenges and move to new levels in your life, business, and relationships.

Everyone I have ever told my story to has been

amazed by it. Sharing the positive aspects of my story have brought me joy, and reminded me how happy I am that I survived. Talking about it in the beginning was both overwhelming and emotional. I would have to lay down afterwards, because it brought upon other symptoms that I didn't understand at the time. It was a roller coaster ride. Writing this book has been mostly enjoyable, as I never thought that I would or could write a book. At the same time, this has also been difficult. I have had to spend time on certain aspects of my story that I would like to forget. It stirs everything back up again, which brings on anxiety.

I chose to write this book and tell people about my story for a few reasons. I hope my story will help people to look past their own adverse circumstances. I also believe everyone has a story worth telling, and looking for the silver linings can be therapeutic. I was motivated to write this book for my own self-healing, but the miraculous and positive aspects of my story seem to help other people touched by traumatic events. Telling this story helps me—and them—to let go of those helpless feelings.

Ultimately, motivation must come from within each person, and that is the main purpose of this book—to spark your inner motivation. I hope my story will provide encouragement, support, and inspiration to help you recognize who you are. I hope it will help you to find your own way forward by making the best use of your own strengths and abilities.

I am proud that I have found inside of me the capacity to create, to overcome, to endure, to transform, and to empower. I strive to be greater than my suffering.

My primary goal is to help others tap into their potential by telling their own stories. This is why I created Story Academy: a step-by-step process for developing your own compelling story, a story that will keep your listeners mesmerized.

If you only had the time to share one idea with someone, what would it be? If they were to leave and forget everything else you said, what would they remember?

You can learn how to keep your story, presentation, or whatever else you want to share engaging and inspiring. Telling your story from the heart creates a connection with your audience. They will feel more comfortable and relaxed because you have opened yourself up and allowed yourself to show some vulnerability. They can now relate to you on another level.

Vince Lombardi said, *"The measure of who we are is what we do with what we have."* My circumstances do not control me... I control my circumstances.

The real story is yours. Good or bad, everyone's life story is different and amazing. Our world and possibilities are endless, so we each have to start telling our own story.

Now, go and tell your story to empower yourself and others.

I would love to share my story with your group. Please reach out and connect with me through www.storyacademy.

14

From Surviving to Thriving

"My mission in life is not merely to survive, but to thrive; and to do so with some passion, some compassion, some humor, and some style."
Maya Angelou

I am now disabled, but I am not going to let that word define me. I have not lost my spirit. I have found renewed confidence and resolve because of what I have overcome to get here. I want people to know that you should always keep pushing forward and never give up. Life is too important.

I have found out that on average, 1,000,000 Canadians injure themselves at work every year ("Occupational Injuries," 2013). This statistic was somewhat alarming to me. Those injuries can cause grievous financial and emotional impacts on workers and their families. When a worker is injured, their life changes. They and their families will have to make many adjustments in the time that lies ahead.

Supporting injured workers only makes sense.

But sadly, there is not enough easily accessible support available. If you are an injured worker, it is natural to feel overwhelmed. It can be helpful to understand that you are not alone. Collaborating with others is sometimes the only resource you have, but it can also be the most rewarding.

Recovering from a catastrophic injury is a path with many steps, hurdles, and setbacks. You should seek out others who can be supportive in this process. The importance of being able to communicate your needs and wants is key towards recovery. Understand it is you who will have to do most of the work to move forward. You will need to seek sources of training, education, and various support services to help you along the way. Also understand that everyone copes with stress in different ways, so find your way, and employ those strategies daily.

Traumatic events are life changing. I had to ask myself, *how can I possibly change my current reality?* I had to focus on what I could do and not what I couldn't do any longer. I had to constantly remind myself that my confidence and pride would increase when I started to manage the challenges that I would face on a daily basis. I had to allow myself to be vulnerable and grow with patience. I then found myself becoming a little stronger, and the struggle started to ease.

If you could do one thing for the rest of your life, what would it be? It took me almost 40 years and a traumatic accident before I found my passion.

I want to help others understand they are not alone, and ultimately I want to help others not have to go through what I have. That is the difference I want to make.

Some people think things happen for a reason, others do not. Some things just happen whether we like it or not and we still have to deal with them. The bottom line is we have a choice in how we are going to deal with our circumstances. Make your life worth watching, because one day it may flash before your eyes.

Studies have shown that mastery of your work, creativity, competence, self-esteem, and optimism are all results of inspiration. People who are inspired and seek out inspiration are more likely to achieve their goals and do so with less effort.

We have to evaluate ourselves from within when seeking out inspiration. What inspires me may not inspire you. Unfortunately, creating inspiration isn't quite as easy as evaluation can be, because you can make judgments both subconsciously and consciously.

The following paragraph was taken from the Harvard Business Review article titled, Why Inspiration Matters:

> *In a culture obsessed with measuring talent and ability, we often overlook the important role of inspiration. Inspiration awakens us to new possibilities by allowing us to transcend our ordinary experiences and limitations. Inspiration propels a person from apathy to possibility,*

and transforms the way we perceive our own capabilities. Inspiration may sometimes be overlooked because of its elusive nature… but as recent research shows, inspiration can be activated, captured, and manipulated, and it has a major effect on important life outcomes. (Kaufman, 2011)

Start creating inspiration by doing something new and creative. It doesn't matter what it is. You can make some art, watch a documentary, or learn something new. The important thing to remember is to expand. Don't keep doing the same thing. My suggestion is to develop and tell your own story, and then allow inspiration to come to you from others as you compare experiences.

Can you say that you understand the fundamental difference between thriving and surviving? Surviving is merely remaining alive, while thriving is growing vigorously or realizing a goal despite adverse circumstances. Based on those definitions, I am sure most of us would easily choose thriving over surviving at any given moment.

So I have two questions for you. Number one, are you in search of something different, something greater? Chances are, if you are not happy with where you are currently then you might be interested in a change. Change can be created out of survival and change can be achieved by thriving. So my second question is: what is the difference between the two?

When you have a survival state of mind you will approach life with the main intention of staying alive, staying on course, holding onto what you have, and you will pursue paths with the least resistance. You will stand around and wait for external variables to shift.

When you have a thriving state of mind you will not just react to your challenges. You will confront your challenges with the intention of turning them into opportunities. You can also try to promote change in your environment. You will cause an external reaction as opposed to just reacting internally. (Kaufman, 2011)

I have to admit that there were times I saw my mere survival as good enough. But it is in that time of struggle that you must invest the most. Invest in yourself and in the tools that can help you achieve your overall goals.

Here are some other important points to remember:

- Do not allow what happens externally to impact how you view yourself and your obstacles internally.
- There cannot be progress without change.
- Respect the mistakes and errors that come along with that change, because those can actually lead to your progress.
- Learn how to take advantage of the difficult situations in order to re-evaluate, learn, and identify valuable lessons.
- Try to always move away from the mindset of "mere survival".

- Finally, seek innovative ways to create new opportunities. (Kaufman, 2011)

I have routinely accomplished things others thought would be impossible. I had the strength in my mind that superseded doubt in the minds of others. I had to start by doing the necessary, to move from breathing to walking. After I took those baby steps, the possible opened up. I had a reason to keep getting out of bed and trying to improve a little bit every day. By making that my routine, and working through my many failures, other doors opened up. Eventually, I was doing what seemed impossible.

As part of my healing process, I hope to inspire others to improve their physical and mental health by developing strategies for thriving. This is not easy, but the most important things in life are worth fighting for. I believe life is for enjoying, having fun, and laughing a lot. You must meet your daily challenges to get to that joyful place. Trust me when I say that I understand that life can bring you down at times. But be grateful, stay positive, and keep learning and you'll get to where you want to go.

Together we will do more than survive...we will thrive!

About The Author

"With every experience, you alone are painting your own canvas, thought by thought, choice by choice."
Oprah Winfrey

I want to share with you a little bit about myself. I am currently 46 years old and as mentioned, I am a husband and father to the best wife and kids anyone could ask for. They are my strength and motivation. They mean the world to me and I am a better person because of them. I could not have overcome what I did without their support. They complete me.

I am out-going, personable, and enjoy the company of others. I feed off others' energy and have enjoyed making people laugh throughout the years. I personally love public speaking and large crowds.

When I was younger, I was involved in music. I played the violin for over 14 years, which included playing in a youth orchestra. I won many awards and scholarships, but music was not my passion. Don't get me wrong, I enjoy all types of music and find it relaxing. I just had other creative interests I wanted to explore more.

My parents wanted all their kids to play music and had certain expectations that were different from mine. I really needed to find my own niche. Unfortunately, I did not have the greatest family support growing up. There was a lot of dysfunction in my family. To make a long story short, some things were a lot harder than they had to be. I had to find support outside my home. I needed to surround myself with people who understood and accepted me.

One of those escapes for me was being involved in a youth group. I was a youth leader through my later teens and early twenties at Christian Life Assembly, (CLA). I met so many great people and those friendships and memories will last a lifetime. As mentioned earlier in the book, this is where I met the Dunkley's. My home away from home, and where I could truly be myself. They brought me out of my protective shell.

Another escape for me was the stage. I loved speaking and acting in front of large crowds of people. I understand that is a huge fear for a lot of people, but not me. CLA put on the most extravagant illustrated sermons, and I would act in most of those. I was given the "out of the box" parts that no-one else wanted. This allowed me to face some of my fears on what I considered, the safe place of the stage. I could step away from, and forget for a moment, the difficulties that were off the stage. I allowed myself to escape into those stories.

My passion growing up was sports. I always found the time to play and watch numerous sports. As a kid, I played hockey and baseball almost every day. But I was most drawn to football. In my opinion, it is the ultimate team game. It teaches all the good qualities you want to demonstrate in life and business. I was so intrigued by the inner "chess match" between defense and offence, and by how eleven people have to play as one to succeed. My wife and I were actually married in a football stadium, on the 50 yard line of the Oakland Alameda County Coliseum. I am a huge Raiders fan so it was my dream wedding.

Throughout the last 12 years before my accident, I coached my kids' baseball and football teams, making many connections in the community along the way. I loved trying to motivate the different kids to get the most out of them. One of the most rewarding things to me is seeing these kids grow up to be amazing young adults. It is touching that a lot of them still call me "Coach" to this day. I was also the PA announcer for my son's high school football team.

I knew I always liked public speaking growing up and a lot of people told me I was a natural. I also excelled in those situations in University, and have performed as a master of ceremonies for many events in the community. My accident has brought me full circle and has revealed to me my purpose, which in turn has led me to my new passion. To help and inspire others to overcome their own challenges. I also want to motivate others to tell their own story and share it with others. Everyone has a story worth telling!

I am now a motivational speaker and co-creator of Story Academy, and the podcast, Surviving to Thriving.

I look forward to connecting with you further. Here are the links to my websites:

www.StoryAcademy.ca
www.SurvivingtoThriving.ca
www.MiracleinaMill.com

I hope you have enjoyed the miraculous story of my near-fatal traumatic accident and the challenges I have overcome to get where I am today. I hope my story has inspired you to live your own life with more purpose. Motivational stories have the capacity to lift us up, make us grin, encourage us, and teach us worthy life lessons. They grant us an empowering feeling of expectancy: "If he or she can do it, then so can I!" Never forget that, there's a lot of truth in that statement.

I love this quote by Margaret J. Wheatley. She said; *"Without reflection, we go blindly on our way, creating more unintended consequences, and failing to achieve anything useful."*

Remember, you cannot reach what is in front of you, until you can let go of what is behind you! We are not given things that we can't handle.

Thank you!

Paul Henczel, BBA, Author, Motivational Speaker and Creator of Story Academy and Surviving to Thriving.

"A story is a journey that moves the listener, and when the listener goes on that journey they feel different and the result is persuasion and sometimes action."
Jennifer Aaker

References

Hitzman, Sue. (2013). The MELT Method to Naturally End Your Pain. Retrieved from: http://www.doctoroz.com/videos/melt-method-naturally-end-your-pain

Hitzmann, Sue. (2013). The MELT Method: A Breakthrough Self-Treatment System to Eliminate Chronic Pain, Erase the Signs of Aging, and Feel Fantastic in Just 10 Minutes a Day. New York City. Longevity Fitness.

Robinson, G., & Rose, M. (2007). Teams for a new generation: A facilitator's field guide. Bloomington, IN: AuthorHouse.

Positive thinking: Stop negative self-talk to reduce stress. (2014). Retrieved from: http://www.mayoclinic.org/healthy-lifestyle/stress-management/in-depth/positive-thinking/art-20043950

Occupational Injuries and Diseases in Canada, 1996-2008. (2013). Retrieved from: http://www.labour.gc.ca/eng/health_safety/pubs_hs/oidc.shtml

Kaufman, Scott B. (2011). Creativity: Why Inspiration Matters. Retrieved from: https://hbr.org/2011/11/why-inspiration-matters

Helper, Dr. S. (2012). Independent Medical Examination for Paul Henczel

Dhawan, Dr. P. (2015). Medical Legal Opinion for Paul Henczel

Schmidt, Dr. J. P. (2014). Neuropsychological Assessment and Medical Legal opinion for Paul Henczel

Bos, D. (2014). Medical Report for Paul Henczel

Dhawan, Dr. P. (2014). Consultation Report for Paul Henczel

Made in the USA
Charleston, SC
11 August 2016